Minute
HISTORY
of the
DRAMA

..{ FROM ITS EARLIEST BEGINNINGS
TO THE PRESENT DAY }..

by

ALICE BUCHANAN FORT

and

HERBERT S. KATES

GROSSET & DUNLAP
Publishers
NEW YORK

CONTENTS

MINUTE HISTORY OF THE DRAMA

From Its Earliest Beginnings to the Present Day

Egypt

The world's earliest report of a dramatic production comes from the banks of the Nile. It is in the form of a stone tablet preserved in a German museum and contains the sketchy description of one, I-kher-nefert, a representative of the Egyptian king, of the parts he played in a performance of the world's first recorded "Passion" Play somewhere around the year 2000 B.C. This Egyptian Passion bears a notable resemblance to the Passion Plays of the twentieth century. Its purpose is obviously the same as that of the one at Ober-Ammergau, or the Tyrolean, or the Persian Passion Play of Hussein . . . the principal object, as always, being to keep vivid in the minds of the faithful the sufferings and triumph of a god.

In the case of the Egyptian "Passion" the central figure was the legendary king-divinity, Osiris. According to the historical legend, Osiris ruled wisely. He was treacherously murdered and his body was cut in pieces and scattered. His wife, Isis, and his son, avenged his murder, gathered up the pieces of his body for pilgrimage relics, won back his throne and established the cult of Osiris-worship. We

Ruins of the Theatre of Dionysus at Athens, Greece

know that Passion plays in his memory were performed annually at Abydos, Busiris, Heliopolis, and elsewhere.

The acting of those days must certainly have been quite as realistic as that on any modern stage, for later Greek historians tell us that many actor-warriors died of the wounds received in the "sham" battles between the enemies of Osiris and the forces led by his son, Ap-uat. The play closes with the resurrection of Osiris as a god and the foreshadowing to all the faithful of their own final resurrection.

Greece

The Greeks had a word for it. In fact, they had two words . . . "tragos," which is Greek for "goat" and "ode" meaning song, and from the combination they made the equivalent of our word, "tragedy," although it is doubtful if at the very first the word carried the same implication that it acquired later.

To go back a bit . . . the everyday life of the Greeks was inextricably bound up with their religion. Thus it was inevitable that their first instinct toward acting should come through the celebration of a festival honoring some one of their innumerable deities. To the Greek people as a whole the fertility of the soil was of tremendous importance; of all their harvests they probably set most store by vintage time. Thus in time it came about that they honored the god of wine, Dionysus, (or Bacchus) with songs and dancing in which all the people took part. Presently as the celebration took on more and more the character of a ritual a certain few were charged with the proper conduct of it, while the rest became the audience. Then, according to tradition, it occurred to one with more "advanced" ideas that it would be something new and spectacular if, instead of having the story of the god told in song by the chorus, an "actor" should act out his story in a dialogue with the leader of the chorus. Semi-legendary history says that the name of that advanced thinker was Thespis . . . and thus was born the Thespian art.

We do not know whether the term "goat song" came from the sacrifice of a goat during the ritual; because goat skins were worn by followers of Dionysus; or because a goat was the

Theatre Marcello, Rome

prize in those very early days to the poet who composed the best play honoring the god. From the middle of the sixth century B.C. history gives us fairly clear records of the Attic celebrations in honor of Dionysus and from then on the record of Athenian drama becomes the history of drama for all Greece. About the middle of this century a regular "theater" was built for the celebrations in honor of Dionysus. This was situated on the southeastern slope of the Acropolis (its ruins remain to this day), and it was there that the annual City Dionysia was held and where Æschylus, Sophocles, and Euripides competed for first prize with plays that had gradually come to have little connection with the god in whose honor the contest originated.

At first these plays were in groups of four, the first three dealing generally with a single theme, tragic in character, and the fourth, a satyr-drama, sometimes dealing with the theme of the first three but treating it more in the manner of a farce. This was in the nature of a sop to the more ignorant classes who missed the boisterous carryings on of the early Dionysian celebrations and doubtless constantly complained that the festivals were getting too "highbrow."

Even at that early day the Greek dramatists had "angels," for each year one of the wealthier and more influential citizens of Athens was appointed to bear the expense of that season's Dionysia, an honor as much sought after as that of chairman of the board of the Metropolitan Opera. The early Greeks had their dramatic critics, too, and even in the fifth century B.C. such a renowned critic as Aristotle found cause to complain of the "star" system. Already, it seems, dramatists were writing their plays with consideration for the talents of the people who were to act them. Already there were comedies satirizing current political situations such as the Pulitzer-Prize-winner, *As Thousands Cheer*, did some twenty-four centuries later for Broadway. And already dramatists wrote with one eye on the box office (in their case, first prize at the City Dionysia) and the other on the "bald-headed row." What those early comedies lacked in pretty girls (all the actors were men) they frequently made up in the ribaldry of their jokes.

Rome

Shortly after the middle of the third century B.C. it became evident that Greece as a political and military power was no longer of great importance, and equally evident that her place was to be taken by Rome. Greek culture, however, had already spread to the bounds of the civilized world, chiefly through the conquests of Alexander the Great.

The Romans were practical men of affairs . . . good politicians, crafty generals, keen analysts . . . but they were adaptors and imitators, not originators. The story of Roman drama is the history of three names: Plautus, an Umbrian peasant who wrote in the third century, B.C.; Terence, a Carthaginian slave, who wrote in the second century, B.C.; and Seneca, born in Cordova, Spain, who wrote in the first century of the Christian era. The first two writers adapted Greek comedy; the latter rewrote Greek tragedies which were probably never acted on any stage, for the Roman stage of that first century A.D. was indescribably rough and vulgar. Seneca's tragedies with their long and flowery speeches could scarcely have held a Roman audience who wanted even the swift-moving comedies of Plautus accompanied by bear-baiting and gladiatorial combats.

With the advent of the Christian era two forces combined for the destruction of drama . . . a natural decay from its own rottenness and that of the times, and an understandable tendency on the part of the new religion to frown upon an institution that owed its origin to the worship of heathen deities. For some eight centuries or more, through what is known

Chinese Theatre

to history as the "Dark Ages," the spirit of drama lay dormant. The wonder is that any of the plays of those early Greeks and their Roman imitators were preserved for the gradual awakening in the Middle Ages of an interest in dramatic expression which came to its full flowering in the various countries of Europe in that period known as the Renaissance.

India

Meanwhile, quite independently of any western civilization drama was born in the East. Of its early beginnings we know little but somewhere around 400 A.D. a Hindu genius, named Kalidasa, wrote the masterpiece of Hindu drama, *Shakuntala*. It is, like most of the Hindu plays, a simple little love lyric with a happy ending, bespeaking an entirely different type of mind and culture than either the comedies or the tragedies of the Greeks. It unfolds a tale so simple that it might be out of a child's fairy tale book, but it is utterly delightful in the telling. The only similarity the play bears to Greek drama is the fact that a curse is responsible for the temporary unhappiness, but it does not, as in the Greek, end in tragedy for all concerned.

The only other Hindu drama worthy of note is *The Little Clay Cart* attributed, whether rightly or wrongly, to a perhaps legendary king, Shudraka. This play, while not so typical, was performed in New York in the Neighborhood Theater during the season of 1924–25. Thus the Golden Age of Hindu Drama, which extended roughly from 400 to 900 A.D. while western drama lay in complete oblivion, came

to a close without exerting any influence on either drama or culture outside its native India.

China

Not until the eighteenth century did any knowledge of the Chinese drama come to the western world and even now there are very few translations. It is not strange, however, to find that modern Chinese drama is almost identical with the drama of China's Golden Age, the twelfth and thirteenth centuries A.D.

There are certain definite concepts to which Chinese drama more or less rigidly adheres. For example, the theory of the Chinese drama is that every play should have a moral. Also, there is that unalterable rule that demands a happy ending. If the happy ending cannot be brought about naturally, it comes through the intervention, not of the gods as in Greek or Hindu drama, but of the Emperor. It is, however, unlawful to represent the person of the Emperor on the stage. The best Chinese plays generally show a regard for unity of plot. Chinese drama, on the whole, shows a much wider range of subject matter than that of either India or Greece. National customs and even Buddhism, the religion of nearly four-fifths of the nation, is held up to ridicule on the stage.

The theory of Chinese stagecraft makes far more demand on the imagination of the audience than did even the scenery-less stage of Shakspere's day. The property man wanders around the stage at will during the performance, furnishing the actors with whatever they require. Since he is dressed in black he is regarded by a Chinese audience as invisible.

From all the history of Chinese drama, there are only three plays that are known to any extent in Europe and America. *The Little Orphan of the House of Tchao* was declared by Voltaire to be a masterpiece far superior to anything produced in Europe prior to the fourteenth century. In fact, he promptly appropriated its plot for a play of his own called *L'Orphelin de Chine*. *The Story of the Magic Lute* is also supposed to date from about the fourteenth century A.D. *The Sorrows of Han*, on the other hand, is said to date from before the Christian era. It is this latter play that is most familiar to the western world. It was staged in New York in 1910 with Miss Edith Wynne Matthison in the cast.

Japan

Regarding plot sources and methods of production Japanese drama is much the same as

Japanese Theatrical Scene from a Hokuyei Print

Chinese. There were, however, in Japan, two distinct types of drama . . . the aristocratic and the popular. It is the aristocratic drama . . . the *No-play* . . . that mostly concerns us. The word "No" corresponds to our term "drama" in the larger sense. The purpose of the *No-play* is not, as in occidental drama, to tell a story or reveal a dramatic situation, but merely to create an image. There is one important difference between the Japanese *No-play* and the Chinese drama. The content of the *No-play* is nearly always tragic.

The *No-play* has a chorus of six men who squat on the stage during the action of the play and serve the same function as the Greek chorus, that of instructor to the audience. Only those Japanese studied in the culture and literature of their country can actually appreciate a *No-play* because of the innumerable allusions

and plays on words which go to make up the play.

According to tradition the popular theater in Japan dates from the early part of the seventeenth century when the priestess, Okuni, ran away from the Shinto temple and built a theater in Kioto. This theater developed in two ways . . . as a "legitimate" show with living actors, and as a marionette or puppet show. At first apparently the nobility attended the popular theater. Evidently as later in France and England there were quarrels and disturbances in the audience which resulted in an edict forbidding the wearing of swords in the theater. The Samurai (knights) preferred to stay away from the theater rather than lay aside their swords even for so short a time, and thereafter the popular theater deteriorated rapidly.

Drama of the Middle Ages

Through practically a thousand years while the European theater was "dark" the Christians were unable to stamp out completely the festive element among the common people that manifested itself particularly at the spring planting time and the harvest season. It is probable, had not the church itself responded to the primitive desire of the people to "act out" the stories of their lives, that secular drama would have sprung up in place of the Mystery, Miracle and Morality plays of the Middle Ages.

It must be remembered, too, that everywhere the service of the church was conducted in Latin rendering it quite unintelligible to the masses of the people. If they were to be familiar with the stories of the Bible that knowledge must come to them through the medium of a portrayal of events in the life of Christ and of his saints. When the early attempts were made by the priests to act out the stories of the

Stage for Valenciennes Mystery Play, 16th Century

Italian Comedy Scene of the 16th Century

Christmas and the Easter seasons, there was little or no national consciousness in continental Europe. It was, to all intents and purposes, one vast domain living under a feudal system and acknowledging a nominal allegiance first to Charlemagne and later to the "Holy Roman Emperor of the German people." There was, too, but one religion. This religious and political unity made it extremely easy for the ideas of the Mystery and Miracle plays to spread through the agency of the bards and troubadors that wandered from court to court of the feudal barons.

At first only the priests took part in acting out the events from the lives of Christ and the saints and the portrayal took place in the church proper. Later as the performances grew more elaborate and space became an important item the Mysteries and Miracles were pushed out into the courtyards of the churches and laymen began to take part in the acting.

By the beginning of the twelfth century national boundaries were becoming more or less marked. England by its geographical position was isolated from the currents of thought that flowed through continental Europe, and there, as the people took over the responsibility for the acting of the sacred plays, it became the custom to turn individual incidents over to the guilds of the various crafts. Also, there arose a feeling of need to present, not only isolated incidents or groups of related incidents at

Christmas and Easter, but the whole history of man from his creation to the day of judgment. The various incidents of this long story were divided among the guilds of a district, staged on wagons easily drawn from one place to another, and were presented in proper sequence at set stations throughout the district. This complete history enacted by the various guilds came to be referred to as a "cycle" and for further identification was referred to by the name of the district in which it was presented. Viewed from the light of modern times the four most important cycles were those of *Chester, York, Coventry,* and *Towneley* (also called *Wakefield*). That these cycles, even though religious in nature, took into account the popular love of comedy is evidenced by the fact that in the only surviving incident of the *Newcastle* cycle Noah's wife is represented as a vixen.

About the same time, both in England and on the continent, the idea was conceived of representing the Virtues and Vices by name in the persons of actors, to afford the audience a "moral" lesson. From this grew the Moralities of which the most famous are the English *Castell of Perseverance* and *Everyman* . . . the latter presumably an import from Holland.

Both the Mystery and the Morality plays were always long winded and frequently dull. To relieve the tedium "interludes" were presented which were nothing more nor less than slapstick farces as a rule more distinguished for their vulgarity than their humor. Most of these farces came originally from France or Italy and dealt either with the subject of sex or of digestion. At their best, however, they carry on the true tradition of the Greek comedy writers and the Roman Plautus and Terence. From these "interludes" (literally "between the games," which was their actual use in Italy) developed a swift moving farce that was acted independently of any other performance. The best and most famous of these farces of the Middle Ages is the French *Farce of Pierre Pathelin.*

National Drama before 1700

Italy

Rising from the ashes of the Mysteries and Miracles in the various countries a feeling for secular drama developed along truly national lines. As early as the fourteenth century in Italy the plays of Plautus and Terence and Seneca began to be revived on the Italian stage. By the first half of the sixteenth century Italian

Outdoor Theatre at Versailles at the time of Louis XIV

writers were making their own adaptations and, following the example of Gian Giorgio Trissino and his tragedy, *Sophonisba*, writing their own plays.

In comedy the most famous names of the period are those of Machiavelli, Ariosto, and Aretino. Italian comedy, even the best of it, exhibited a dreadful sameness filled with stock characters . . . the braggart soldier; the aged husband invariably deceived by the young wife; the tricky servant, and so on through a long list, which the audience recognized in the moment of their appearance by their costumes. About eight times out of ten these comedies made use of the kidnapping theme.

But another type of play, also, had its birth in Italy during the late sixteenth century. The first important example of this new pastoral drama was Torquato Tasso's *Aminta*, a play which not only had pretty costumes and delightful music, but also great literary beauty. Within twenty years Guarini, an imitator of the celebrated Tasso, had written his *Pastor Fido*, which, although less beautiful, has more life than its model.

Spain

In Spain during the sixteenth century there was some attempt at imitation of the Italian drama by the Cervantes of *Don Quixote* fame. About the middle of the century, however,

Lope de Rueda, a gold beater of Seville, became the leader of a band of strolling players. In his more or less extemporaneous plays he ridiculed his fellow citizens with a good-humored shrewdness that has sometimes caused him to be regarded as the real founder of the Spanish drama.

Almost contemporary with him, however, was Lope de Vega, the prolific playwright who ushered in Spain's Golden Age of drama which was to end so very shortly with his contemporary-successor, Calderon. The rise of a truly national drama in Spain has exceptional importance because of its influence on the work of later French dramatists . . . notably Molière, Corneille, and Voltaire.

France

In France there were before the seventeenth century a few sporadic attempts to establish a national drama but for the most part the sixteenth century was devoted to copies and adaptations of the Senecan patterns of the classics. Then shortly after the beginning of the seventeenth century Pierre Corneille was born, and in 1637 his drama, *The Cid*, established him as the acknowledged leader of the French dramatic movement.

Two years after the production of *The Cid*, Jean Racine was born, and in 1667 this newcomer successfully challenged Corneille's leadership with his highly popular *Andromaque*. This drama represented a principle of composition fundamentally different from that of Corneille . . . a principle that was also subscribed to by the greatest comedy writer of France and of the Christian era, Molière, who likewise belongs to seventeenth century France.

England

In England early in the sixteenth century the interlude served as a base for the early comedy writers. John Heywood was the best known writer of interludes and *The Four P's* his best known work. Nicholas Udall, the first writer of comedies, brought to the English stage the *Miles Gloriosus* of Plautus in his *Ralph Roister Doister*. *Gammer Gurton's Needle*, the second native comedy (authorship undetermined), is a more original farce built entirely around local types. The first distinctly English tragedy, also a product of this period, was *Gorboduc*, performed before Queen Elizabeth in 1561.

The latter part of the sixteenth century brought to England the greatest glory she was to

have, for following close on the production of
Thomas Kyd's *Spanish Tragedy* and Christopher
Marlowe's *Tamburlaine* came Shakspere's early
plays and by the close of the century he was
acknowledged leader of a not inconsiderable
group of English geniuses. Shakspere's most
important work came during the last sixteen
years of his life (1600–1616) and for that time he
overshadowed figures that would otherwise have
stood out even more importantly than they
did: Thomas Heywood with his domestic
tragedy *A Woman Killed with Kindness;* the prolific Ben Jonson; the famous collaborators,
Beaumont and Fletcher; Massinger, Dekker and
a host of others.

During the latter part of the seventeenth
century the Puritans under Cromwell succeeded
in closing the theaters for eighteen years (1642–
1660). When, under the Stuarts of the Restoration, the theaters were reopened it was to an
entirely different and inferior type of play.
True, the plays of the Elizabethan days were
still performed, but the influence of the French
school was felt more and more. Such English
drama as was produced had lost its homely
virility and retained little more than cleverness
and bombast. Of the names of this period,
Dryden, Otway, Etherege, Wycherley, Con-
greve, VanBrugh, and Farquhar are remembered by students of literature and drama.

Soon after the Restoration women began to
appear in the English theater, both as actresses
and as playwrights. But the stage of the
Restoration, vulgar though it undoubtedly was,
and weak by comparison with its Elizabethan
glory, still did not deserve the scathing condemnation of the clergyman, Jeremy Collier, in his
famous pamphlet published in 1698.

Eighteenth Century

The eighteenth century added little glory to
the national drama so far considered. In
England only two names stand out, those of
Sheridan and Goldsmith, although Addison's
Cato achieved a spectacular popular success.
In France, Voltaire, a disciple of classicism,
achieved a reputation that spread beyond the
bounds of his own country through most of the
European world. In 1775 Beaumarchais enjoyed
an extraordinary success with his *Barber of
Seville*, although today it is better known
through Rossini's opera for which it served as
the libretto. Nine years later the same dramatist
wrote *The Marriage of Figaro*, but this was so
filled with revolutionary sentiment that its

An Early French Traveling Theatre

performance was forbidden. Later it was used
as the libretto for Mozart's opera of the same
name. In Italy there were Goldoni and Alfieri,
and in Spain, no dramatists of any international
importance.

The eighteenth century, however, marked
the dramatic awakening of Germany and
Scandinavia. For Germany, indeed, this century
produced the three greatest names in her dramatic history . . . Lessing, Goethe, and Schiller. In the Scandinavian countries, Ludwig
Holberg alone deserves mention. A native of
Bergen, Norway, Holberg had settled in Copenhagen, the literary center of Scandinavia.
King Frederick IV, not particularly pleased with
the foreign plays that found their way to
Copenhagen's single theater, invited Holberg
to try his hand, so successfully, as it turned out,
that he earned the title of "Father of Danish
Literature."

Nineteenth Century

In the late eighteenth and early nineteenth
centuries, the outstanding movement in the
dramatic field was that of romanticism as
against the classicism of most earlier European
drama. In France, the nineteenth century
added the names of Victor Hugo, Eugène Scribe,
Émile Augier, Alexander Dumas, the Younger,
and Victorien Sardou.

In England a literary or "closet" drama,
entirely unsuited to stage production, sprang up.
It listed in its annals such names as Words-
worth, Coleridge, Byron, Shelley, Swinburne,
Browning, and Tennyson. It was not until the
latter part of the century that the English stage

Old John Street Theatre, New York, 1767-1798

again showed signs of life with the advent of Henry Arthur Jones, Sir Arthur Wing Pinero, and Oscar Wilde.

The latter part of this century, too, saw the beginning of the independent theater movement that was to be the forerunner of the "Little Theater" movement that in the twentieth century spread far and wide. It was in such theaters as these . . . the *Théâtre Libre* of Paris, *Die Freie Bühne* of Berlin, the *Independent Theater* of London and *Miss Horniman's Theater* in Manchester, that Ibsen, Strindberg, Björnson, Yeats, Shaw, Hauptmann and Synge were first given a hearing.

During the latter part of the century in Germany there appeared two dramatists who since the turn of the century have won international fame . . . Hauptmann and Sudermann. A Viennese physician, Arthur Schnitzler, has become widely known outside his native Austria through his light and amusing *Anatol*.

In France, Brieux became the herald of a realistic, not to say clinical, drama. Belgium produced a Maeterlinck. But the most notable event of the late nineteenth century was probably the production in Paris of Edmond Rostand's *Cyrano de Bergerac*.

It is, after that, something of an anti-climax to record that in Italy Giacosa was writing his best known play, *As the Leaves*, and composing the librettos for the operas, *La Bohème*, *Tosca*, and *Madame Butterfly;* or that Verga wrote *In the Porter's Lodge*, *The Fox Hunt*, and *Cavalleria Rusticana*, which again is better known through Mascagni's opera; or even that the best known of nineteenth century Italian

dramatists, Gabriel d'Annunzio, was making his somewhat contradictory contributions to dramatic art. Of the Italians who began their work in the late nineteenth century, two deserve mention in connection with the present century, Luigi Pirandello who has a chapter of his own, and Sem Benelli whose *Supper of Jokes* is known on the English and American stage as *The Jest*. Benelli's *Love of the Three Kings* is best known outside Italy in its operatic form.

In Spain José Echegaray, author of *The World and His Wife;* José Benavente, whose *Passion Flower* and *Bonds of Interest* have recently been offered on the American stage; and the brothers Sierra whose *Cradle Song* achieved international fame, are a connecting link between the nineteenth and twentieth centuries, as are Shaw, Galsworthy, and Barrie in England and Lady Augusta Gregory and W. B. Yeats in Ireland.

Russian drama has had so little connection with other dramatic movements in Europe that it has seemed wise to give it a page to itself in the book proper. And as for our own century, that is covered, if somewhat briefly, in the two pages titled Drama in the First Quarter of the Twentieth Century and The Stage of Today and Tomorrow.

Drury Lane Theatre, London

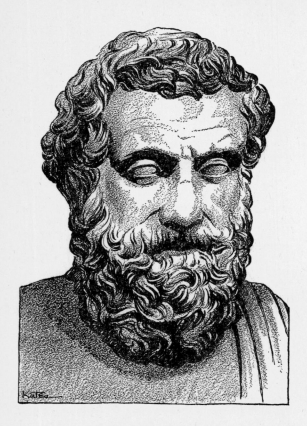

AEschylus

Father of Greek Drama

..{ *Born, Eleusis, Greece, 525 B.C.* }..
 { *Died, Syracuse, Sicily, 456 B.C.* }

IN THE lives of the three great Greek trage-
dians, tradition is so mixed with fact, and
the facts themselves frequently so uncertain, that
it is hard to tell where one leaves off and the
other begins. According to tradition the great
service of Æschylus to Greek drama had its beginnings in a dream. One night when he was
watching his father's flocks, the gods in a vision commanded him to write tragic dramas for
their glorification in the religious festivals.

Whether there is anything of truth in the
story or not, Æschylus must have begun writing
plays at an early age for we find him when
scarcely twenty-five years old competing in the
dramatic contests held yearly in honor of the
god, Dionysus. It was fifteen years, however,
before he carried off first prize. Meanwhile, he
had learned his craft so well that from his first
success in 484 B.C. he continued to win almost
continuously until his death.

The parents of Æschylus belonged to the old
Attic nobility so that family life and traditions
tended to make him a broadminded conserva-
tive, both in politics and religion. The circumstance that his birthplace, Eleusis, was the
center of the worship of the goddess, Demeter,
probably is largely responsible for his keen religious consciousness, and the fact that in all his
extant plays the unvarying motive is the relentless power of Fate and the ultimate justice of
Providence.

Æschylus spent a great part of his mature life
at the court of Hieron, tyrant of Syracuse, returning to Athens to supervise the production of
his dramas for the contests, in which he apparently competed alternate years. He continued to write up to the day of his death which,
according to the story told, was caused by an
eagle's mistaking his bald head for a stone and
dropping a tortoise on it to break the shell.
But this tale we shall have to take with more
than a grain of salt.

Æschylus was the first dramatist to give
dignity and meaning to tragedy. Also, as his
own producer and stage manager, he designed
special costumes for his actors; pioneered in the
use of masks; enlarged the stage; and was the
first dramatist to have any sort of setting for his
plays. Altogether, it is probable that few men
in the entire history of the theater, have had
such far reaching effect on their chosen profession as Æschylus, Father of Greek Drama.

AGAMEMNON

The opening play in the Oresteian Trilogy, which won first place in the City Dionysia in 458 B.C. The Trilogy was completed on that occasion by a satyr-drama, "Proteus," on the same theme, making a tetralogy. "Proteus," however, has been lost.

SCENE: *The Palace of Agamemnon in Argos; statues of the gods in front.*

MORE than ten years before the action of the play begins, Paris, Prince of Troy, had betrayed the hospitality of Menelaus, King of Sparta, by eloping with Menelaus's wife, the beautiful Helen. Menelaus's brother, Agamemnon, King of Argos, had been elected head of the armies promptly assembled from all the Greek cities for the purpose of avenging the injury to Menelaus. For ten long years the Grecian hosts had besieged the walls of Troy, but as the play opens their signal fires announcing Troy fallen and Menelaus avenged have just been sighted by the watchman on the roof of the palace in Argos.

During these ten years Clytæmnestra, Agamemnon's faithless queen, had taken for her lover, Ægisthus, blood enemy of Agamemnon's house. Now when the watchman rushes down from the roof of the palace to wake the sleeping household and to announce the imminent return of the rightful king, Clytæmnestra immediately makes plans for his reception. Almost on the heels of the announcement Agamemnon himself arrives with many captives and loads of booty in his train. Clytæmnestra greets him with great show of wifely affection, has purple tapestries laid for him to walk upon as befits a conqueror, and bids him come within to refresh himself from his travels.

Now among the captives is Cassandra, the seeress daughter of the Trojan King, whom Agamemnon had taken as concubine. Scarcely have Clytæmnestra and Agamemnon entered the palace when Cassandra falls into a trance and foretells the murder of both Agamemnon and herself by the faithless queen. Then she enters the palace from behind whose closed doors almost at once comes a scream and then a dying moan. Shortly the doors are thrown open to reveal the double murder and Clytæmnestra appears to justify her deed before the Argive elders. She reminds them that ten years before Agamemnon had sacrificed her daughter, Iphigenia, to propitiate the gods and gain calm seas for the Grecian fleet. She calls to their attention the fact that he returned home flaunting another woman in her face. Her deed, she claims, is no murder but a just retribution.

The people of Argos, however, have always resented Ægisthus as an interloper. Some of them want to take matters into their own hands and avenge the death of their King. But the wiser heads among them counsel discretion and remind them that in his son, Orestes, now approaching manhood, Agamemnon will shortly find a natural avenger.

CHOËPHORI

("The Libation Pourers")

*The second play in the prize-winning Oresteian Trilogy presented at the City Dionysia in
458 B.C.*

SCENE: *The Palace of Agamemnon in Argos; Agamemnon's tomb in the background.*

THE years pass. The land of Argos seemingly
prospers under the rule of Clytæmnestra and
Ægisthus. The young Orestes has been sent off
to Phocis to make sure that as he grows up he
doesn't take vengeance on Ægisthus for his
father's death. The only one in the palace who
grieves for Agamemnon is his daughter, Electra,
and she dares not mourn him openly.

Clytæmnestra's nights, however, are not as
peaceful as her days. Agamemnon's haunting
spirit keeps her sleepless. Finally, in desperation, she sends Electra with her maidens to pour
offerings of wine on Agamemnon's tomb in
hopes to appease his spirit.

Shortly before Electra and her companions
reach the tomb, a travel-stained stranger appears
there, gazes reverently down upon it, and at
length clips a lock of his hair and lays it on the
tomb. When he sees the crowd coming from the
palace he hides but as soon as their conversation
assures him that they, too, want to see Agamemnon avenged, he comes forth and identifies himself to his sister as her exiled brother, Orestes.

Electra is overjoyed at his arrival and when he
tells her that Apollo has commanded him to kill
both Ægisthus and Clytæmnestra she urges him
on to the deed of vengeance. They plan that in
order to obtain entrance to the palace he shall
claim hospitality as a travel-tired stranger from
Phocis. Just as they expect, Clytæmnestra receives this Phocian stranger eagerly and in
response to her questions Orestes tells her a
trumped-up story of his own death. Hearing
this, she promptly sends for Ægisthus in order
that he may question the stranger more closely
and make sure that the welcome news is truth
and not mere hearsay. Ægisthus is tricked by
the servant sent to summon him into coming

into Orestes's presence without his bodyguard,
whereupon Orestes loses no time in carrying out
Apollo's command.

Now Greek religious beliefs justify the killing of Ægisthus in revenge for the stealing of
Agamemnon's wife and kingdom as well as for
complicity in his murder. But in spite of the
fact that Orestes had acted at the express command of Apollo, the slaying of his mother has
doomed him to pursuit by the terrible avenging
Furies during this life and the life hereafter. As
the play closes the Furies appear in the background, invisible to all save their victim.

EUMENIDES

("The Benign Ones")

This is the third and last of the plays composing the Oresteian Trilogy.

SCENE: *The Oracle of Apollo at Delphi; later the Temple of Athena and the Areopagus at Athens.*

AFTER the murder of Clytæmnestra, the Furies drive Orestes ceaselessly from land to land, making his life miserable. Finally, bloodstained and utterly weary, he arrives at the Oracle of Apollo. Reminding the god that his actions had been taken at Apollo's express command, Orestes throws himself on divine mercy. Apollo commands him to observe all the purification rites demanded by Greek religion and then to appear at the temple of Athena in Athens. The god further assures him that he himself will be there to plead Orestes's case before the goddess of wisdom and justice.

After more wanderings and intense suffering Orestes arrives at Athens, still pursued by the Furies but no longer blood-stained. In response to his plea Athena assures him of a fair trial and goes herself to summon twelve Athenian citizens to act as the jury. With the Furies as complainants and Apollo as lawyer for the defense, Orestes appears before Athena and the jury at the Areopagus, where the Athenian court of justice is held.

Apollo makes a most ingenious defense, claiming that a mother is not really a blood relation and thus Orestes's act did not outrage religion and the gods, but was only the duty of a son to a murdered father. In proof of his point, the god cites the circumstances of Athena's own birth, how she had sprung fully armed from the head of her father, Zeus, and had never known a mother. The Furies present their case and, in spite of Apollo's eloquent plea, the jury is tied. Athena casts the deciding vote in favor of Orestes.

When the case goes against them the Furies in terrible anger threaten to devastate the land with plagues. In alarm, Athena sets to work to placate them. She assures them that if they will settle down peacefully there in Athens, the citizens to show their appreciation will build them a beautiful shrine and worship them as kindly divinities instead of dreading them as scourges. Thus propitiated, the Furies change their character and from this time on are worshipped in Athens as Eumenides or The Benign Ones.

Statuette of Greek Tragic Actor

Sophocles

..{ *Born, Colonus, Attica, 497 B.C.* }..
  { *Died, Athens, 406 B.C.* }

"FEW poets have lived through a more eventful period of history than Sophocles. His career coincided almost exactly with the rise, maturity, and downfall of the Athenian Empire."[1]

Sophocles' father, Sophillus, was not a member of the Attic aristocracy but he was a rich man through the efforts of his slaves who were employed in various sorts of manufacturing. Consequently the boy was educated as was customary for youths of aristocratic family, in dancing and music, coupled with gymnastic instruction. In fact, he was so conspicuous for his beauty of form and for his skill in dancing and music, that he was chosen to lead the chorus of boys in the public celebration of the defeat of the Persians at Salamis.

Sophocles made his first appearance as a contending dramatist at the City Dionysia in 486 B.C. when he was twenty-eight years old, winning a victory over Æschylus. From that time on he generally exhibited every other year and won in all eighteen victories at the City Dionysia besides those won at the Lenæa. His most surprising defeat was with the *Œdipus Tyrannus* which is generally regarded as his masterpiece.

Of the plays presented at these contests only the seven selected for study and general reading in the ancient schools survive. The *Œdipus Rex* (or *Tyrannus*) is a supreme example of unconscious irony and is regarded as the perfection of Greek tragedy. *Œdipus Coloneus* (his last tragedy), *Electra*, and *Antigone*, also rate high and were most popular on the Attic stage. The remaining three—*Ajax*, *Trachiniæ*, and *Philoctetes*—are good but not so well known.

Sophocles' greatness as a dramatic writer consisted not so much in his inventiveness as in his development and rounding out of the dramatic form brought into being by Thespis and Æschylus. He added the third actor and thus pronounced the doom of the chorus as an element of prime importance in Greek tragedy. He abandoned the trilogic form of composition for separate pieces of art.

In the works of Æschylus, the moralist often overshadows the dramatist; in those of Sophocles, dramatic interest always holds first place. His plays are outstanding for their smoothness of plot, the nobility of the characters and the graceful charm of the lyrics. In a sense they might be said to mirror the serenity of the poet's own life. He had a tranquil and contented temperament and a generous spirit free from petty jealousies. He was witty, agreeable, and fond of people and his mind was keen and active right up to the time of his death at the age of 91.

[1] A. E. Haigh in *The Tragic Drama of the Greeks.*

OEDIPUS REX

("OEdipus the King")

Date and circumstances of production unknown. It is, however, known that Sophocles suffered defeat in the contests with this play, although it is generally regarded as his masterpiece.

SCENE: *Courtyard before the palace of OEdipus, king of Thebes, with most of the Theban population gathered there.*

SOME twelve years before the action of the play begins, OEdipus has been made King of Thebes in gratitude for his freeing the people from the pestilence brought on them by the presence of the riddling Sphinx. Since Laius, the former king, had shortly before been killed, OEdipus has been further honored by the hand of Queen Jocasta.

Now another deadly pestilence is raging and the people have come to ask OEdipus to rescue them as before. The King has anticipated their need, however. Creon, Jocasta's brother, returns at the very moment from Apollo's oracle with the announcement that all will be well if Laius's murderer be found and cast from the city.

In an effort to discover the murderer, OEdipus sends for the blind seer, Tiresias. Under protest the prophet names OEdipus himself as the criminal. OEdipus, outraged at the accusation, denounces it as a plot of Creon to gain the throne. Jocasta appears just in time to avoid a battle between the two men. Seers, she assures OEdipus, are not infallible. In proof, she cites the old prophecy that her son should kill his father and have children by his mother. She prevented its fulfillment, she confesses, by abandoning their infant son in the mountains. As for Laius, he had been killed by robbers years later at the junction of three roads on the route to Delphi.

This information makes OEdipus uneasy. He recalls having killed a man answering Laius's description at this very spot when he was fleeing from his home in Corinth to avoid fulfillment of a similar prophecy. An aged messenger arrives from Corinth, at this point, to announce the death of King Polybus, supposed father of OEdipus, and the election of OEdipus as king in his stead. On account of the old prophecy OEdipus refuses to return to Corinth until his mother, too, is dead. To calm his fears the messenger assures him that he is not the blood son of Polybus and Merope, but a foundling from the house of Laius deserted in the mountains. This statement is confirmed by the old shepherd whom Jocasta had charged with the task of exposing her babe. Thus the ancient prophecy has been fulfilled in each dreadful detail. Jocasta in her horror hangs herself and OEdipus stabs out his eyes. Then he imposes on himself the penalty of exile which he had promised for the murderer of Laius.

Euripides

.·{ *Born, Phlya, Attica, 485 B.C.* }·.
·{ *Died, Macedonia, 407–6 B.C.* }··

THERE is more unadulterated gossip about Euripides than about either Sophocles or Æschylus: about his birth, which for the sake of connecting him with the battle of Salamis and thus with the careers of Æschylus and Sophocles, gossip tries to place in 480 B.C.; about his parentage, probably due to scurrilous remarks in the comedies of Aristophanes referring to them as "hucksters" and "green grocers"; about his youth, when, according to unfounded report,

he was trained for a professional wrestler; and, finally, about his marriage wherein rumor represented him as finding both his first and second wives unfaithful. All this can only be ascribed to the fact that ancient biography resorted to invention in order to connect the poet's writings with supposed personal experiences and thus assign a reason for them.

From all the confusion a few facts stand out. Euripides in temperament was just the opposite of Sophocles . . . of a studious and retiring disposition, fond of the companionship of intimate friends, but averse to general society. A favorite retreat was a grotto that looked out upon the sea. Here in complete retirement he liked to study and write. From numerous allusions of contemporary writers, we know, too, that his library was celebrated for its completeness.

Of the three great tragic poets of Greece, Euripides was by far the most modern. As the first of the "realists" he brought realism in clothes, conversation and character to the Greek stage. He was a pioneer in tragi-comedy, *Alcestis* being the first example in dramatic history of the form later perfected by Spanish and Elizabethan dramatists. The lost *Andromeda* was the only play of ancient times based on the romantic affection of a youth for a girl. *Helena* was a forerunner of the type later made famous by *A Midsummer Night's Dream.*

Of the nineteen extant Euripidean dramas some are good; some, second rate. Nine of his plays were selected for reading in the early schools. Although he exhibited quite regularly he was successful in the dramatic contests only five times, once posthumously. Ancients ranked *Bacchæ* and *Iphigenia in Tauris* as his best works. Like Sophocles' *Œdipus Rex*, Euripides' *Medea*, ranked (with *Hippolytus*) as his masterpiece, was defeated in the contest. These two dramas are the greatest and most original of the poet's creations.

Shortly before his death Euripides accepted an invitation from Archelaus, ruler of Macedon. He was generously treated there and at his death buried with honors.

HIPPOLYTUS

Acted at Athens in 429 B.C., bringing its author the first prize. The scene is laid in Trozên.

THE goddess, Aphrodite, is much incensed because Hippolytus, bastard son of King Theseus of Trozên and the Amazon, Hippolyte, worships only the pure Artemis. She resolves, therefore, to bring about his death through the very sex that he has scorned, and scorning, has thus offered insult to the mighty Aphrodite.

For some months past, Phædra, beloved wife of Theseus, has hidden in her inmost heart a secret passion for the manly Hippolytus. Through unsatisfied desire and secret shame she has wasted away until her old nurse despairs of her life. Finally, after much coaxing, the old nurse learns her secret. On pretense of making a love-philter that will cure Phædra of her unholy love, the nurse confesses her mistress's secret to Hippolytus. The latter in anger scorns and upbraids Phædra. Only his oath of secrecy given to the nurse, he admits, keeps him from confessing his step-mother's shame to the King as soon as His Majesty returns.

Phædra, in her half-crazed state, scarcely heeds him. She sees honor gone and her life ruined through her old servant's mistaken kindness, for she really believes that Hippolytus means to tell the King. In despair she hangs herself. Before the dread deed, however, she has written on her tablet, sealed with the royal seal, the charge that Hippolytus has dishonored her. On the King's arrival the first thing he notes is the tablet fastened to his dead wife's wrist. Grief-stricken, he opens it believing that it will contain some final directions for the care of their children, only to be shocked by the terrible accusation against Hippolytus.

The Prince's protestations of innocence are unavailing against the King's unreasoning anger, and his oath prevents his speaking the whole truth. Theseus condemns his son to life-long exile and in addition prays to his ancestor, Poseidon, powerful god of the sea, to destroy this ravisher of his dear wife.

Hippolytus, knowing the futility of further arguments, mounts his chariot to drive along the seashore until he shall reach his father's boundaries. As he drives, a terrible monster, riding a huge wave, so affrights his spirited horses that he is dashed against the rocks and is carried back, dying, to his father's presence. While he is still conscious Artemis appears in a cloud and explains to Theseus how cruelly Aphrodite had plotted against Hippolytus. Thus both the youth and Phædra are revealed as the innocent victims of a goddess's jealousy and their honor is vindicated.

Aristophanes

..{ *Born, probably 448 B.C.* }..
.{ *Died, probably 385, B.C.* }.

THE literary activity of the famous Greek comedy writer, Aristophanes, covered a period of forty years. During that time the telling satire of his pen was brought to bear alike on prominent men, political trends, and social foibles. Of the forty plays known to be genuine products of his genius eleven remain for posterity. But these easily prove that for wit, rollicking humor, invention, and skill in the use of language Aristophanes has never been surpassed.

Of the poet's life we know very little. Even the place of his birth is in doubt. His family, however, evidently had some wealth for the poet's education was obviously of the best. In politics he supported the aristocratic peace party with all the force of an impetuous nature.

Classical commentators have divided the work of Aristophanes into three periods. The first period ended about 421 B.C. and included two of his lost plays as well as five of the surviving ones. For some reason Aristophanes' first three plays were brought out under the name of one of his actors. They included the two lost plays, *The Banqueters* and *The Babylonians*, and the prize-winning *Acharnians*. *The Knights*, which won first prize in 424 B.C., was brought out under the author's own name. It contained a sharp attack on the demagogue, Cleon, and, because no actor was willing to incur the enmity of so powerful a person, Aristophanes had to play the part of Cleon himself.

The Clouds (423 B.C.) contains the famous dialogue scene between the Just and the Unjust argument. *The Wasps* (422 B.C.) ridiculed the regular courts of justice. *The Peace* (421 B.C.) was written in the interests of the recently concluded peace between Athens and Sparta.

During the seven years that passed before Aristophanes exhibited another play, a law had been passed to check political satire. In the second group, beginning with *The Birds* (414 B.C.) he turned to social satire and ridiculed the fondness of the Athenians for litigation. *Lysistrata* (411 B.C.) represents a woman's efforts to bring about peace, while *Thesmophoriazusæ* of the same year contains an attack on Euripides.

The Frogs, which started the third period in 405 B.C. was devoted to literary and dramatic criticism. *Ecclesiazusæ* (*Women in Parliament*) was a satire on current communistic ideas. The local character of the plays of the first period had by the third period given way to a cosmopolitanism that marks Aristophanes as the transition-link between what is termed "Old Comedy" and the "Middle" and "New Comedy" of Greece.

THE FROGS

Probably produced at the Lenæan festival in Athens in January, 405 B.C. where it took first prize. It scored such a hit that it was staged a second time, probably in March of the same year, at the Great Dionysia. It is typical of the lyrical-burlesques of Aristophanes.

SCENE: *Thebes; the nether bank of the Acherusian Lake in Pluto's domain.*

THE god, Dionysus, as a theater goer, bemoans the lack of good contemporary dramatists. This lack, he feels, reflects on the reputation of the yearly celebrations in his own honor. After some consideration he resolves to go with his servant, Xanthias, to the afterworld and bring back that Prince of dramatists, Euripides. With this plan in mind he procures a lion skin and club and disguises himself to represent the recklessly brave Heracles, thinking thus to fortify himself against the dangers of the journey. He makes a final call on the immortal Heracles to ask directions and then sets out.

Dionysus himself is ferried across to Hades by the boatman, Charon, through a chorus of croaking frogs who seem to be pretty well posted on the doings of mortals. Since Charon disdains to ferry Xanthias across the lake the latter has to walk around and meet his master at the entrance to Hades. No sooner are the two inside Pluto's realm than the inhabitants, spying the club and lion skin, decide their chance has come to get even with Heracles for certain misdeeds of that reckless hero on his own visit to the nether world. Dionysus in great alarm insists that his servant change costumes with him, an incident which gives rise to banter of the type indulged in by two modern stage comedians in a musical show. The change is scarcely accomplished, however, when the maid of the lovely Proserpine appears to bid the supposed hero to a banquet. Dionysus insists on reassuming the lion skin that he may accept the invitation, but no sooner has he done so than two indignant eating-house keepers assail the supposed Heracles for damages done on his previous visit. At this point, Dionysus in terror reveals his actual identity.

The news spreads that Dionysus is in Hades and almost at once loud quarreling is heard. The disturbance turns out to be Æschylus and Euripides disputing the place of honor as King of Tragedy, a position which Æschylus holds and Euripides wants. It is finally agreed that since their plays were written for performance at the Dionysian festivals, Dionysus shall decide their dispute. A trial is held and in the end the matter is settled by weighing verses from each poet's writings in the scales. Æschylus as the writer of heavier verses is declared the winner. But the trial has changed Dionysus's mind and he departs for earth taking Æschylus instead of Euripides, leaving Sophocles meanwhile to hold down the place of honor.

DIONYSUS   HERACLES

Titus Maccius Plautus

$$\cdot\cdot\{ \begin{array}{c} \textit{Born, Sarsina, Umbria, probably between} \\ \textit{254–251 B.C.} \\ \textit{Died, probably in Rome, 184 B.C.} \end{array} \}\cdot\cdot$$

"PLAUTUS," the single name by which moderns refer to this writer of Roman comedy, was merely a nickname which in the Umbrian dialect meant "flatfoot." It is exactly as though, today, we were to say, "John Jones, Beanpole."

It is doubtful whether Plautus ever achieved Roman citizenship. He is supposed to have made money working around the Roman stages as carpenter or mechanic; to have set himself up in some sort of business where he promptly lost his entire savings; finally to have been reduced to turning a handmill for a baker. It is during this period, according to tradition that he probably sold his first plays to the managers of the public games and thus began the playwriting career that lasted for nearly forty years.

The plays of Plautus, as was the custom, had Greek characters, Greek names, and Greek scenery, but the manners and flavor were distinctly Roman. Most of his plots Plautus adopted whole from Greek originals of the "New Comedy" period. If we find the comedies of Plautus unspeakably vulgar in conception and expression we must remember that he had to appeal to an uneducated crowd whose chief interests were in bear baiting and gladiatorial combats. If Plautus was to eat, his humor had to be broad or his plays would have been shouted off the stage.

Menæchmi, or *The Twin Brothers*, is probably the best known of the Plautian comedies because it was translated into English at an earlier date than others of his works. It is from this play that Shakspere took the plot for his *Comedy of Errors*. From the Plautian comedy, *Miles Gloriosus (The Braggart Soldier)* the swaggering soldier type of the Renaissance was born while from *Amphytruo* later under Molière's skillful touch came a popular French comedy. Nicholas Udall's *Ralph Roister Doister* also owes its life to Miles Gloriosus as does Shakspere's eternal Falstaff. Jonson's *The Case Is Altered* is a skillful amalgamation of *Aulularia* and *Captivi*. Dryden, Addison, and the German Lessing also profited from plots and characters of Plautus.

The works of Plautus do not show the insight nor delicacy of Terence, but they possess undoubted life and vigor. His originality showed itself in his attempts to set whole scenes to music. His perfect command and skillful use of the Latin language gained for him the favor of the more cultured Romans, just as his swift-moving plots and humorous situations attracted the uneducated classes.

MENAECHMI or THE TWIN BROTHERS

There seems to be no record of the time and circumstances of the production of this play during the time of Plautus. Its earliest revival occurred under the direction of Ercole I, Duke of Ferrara, early in the Middle Ages, probably between 1486 and 1550.

SCENE: *A street in Epidamnus on which front the dwellings of Menæchmus of Epidamnus and of Erotium, the courtesan.*

MOSCHUS, a merchant of Syracuse, had twin sons who were like as two peas. When the boys were seven years old, Moschus took one of them, Menæchmus, with him on a business trip to Tarentum. There the boy became separated from his father and lost in the crowd. He was found and later adopted by a wealthy merchant of Epidamnus. In this city he grew to manhood and married a rich wife.

Meanwhile, so great was the grief of parents and grandparents for the lost boy that the remaining twin whose name was Sosicles was renamed Menæchmus. When the latter reached young manhood he set out with his slave, Messenio, to cover the known world in search of his twin. At the opening of the action, Menæchmus Sosicles and Messenio have just arrived at Epidamnus after six years of wandering.

Just prior to their appearance on the street where Menæchmus of Epidamnus lives, the latter has as usual been quarreling with his wife. To spite her he has stolen a rich mantle of hers to give to the courtesan, Erotium. He requests this lady to prepare a feast for himself and his Parasite, Peniculus, the while they go to the market place to transact some business.

When she sees Menæchmus Sosicles, Erotium insists that he come in and eat the feast she has prepared. When he leaves she gives him the mantle along with a gold bracelet and requests that he have them repaired. Meanwhile, the wife of Menæchmus of Epidamnus discovers the loss of the mantle and makes such a scene that her husband attempts to recover the mantle from Erotium. That lady believes that her patron is trying to put something over on her and retires into her house in a rage leaving Menæchmus dinnerless without.

About this time the wife spies the visiting Menæchmus with her mantle and starts berating him loudly. When he disclaims all knowledge of her she calls her father and some servants to take him in custody, believing he has gone suddenly mad. This impression increases when, with the help of Messenio, Menæchmus spiritedly resists.

Finally the twin brothers are brought face to face but it never seems to occur to Menæchmus Sosicles that here is the twin he has been seeking. It is left for Messenio to unravel the tangle and thus win the gift of freedom. The comedy closes with plans for an auction of all the property of Menæchmus of Epidamnus, including his wife, that he may return with his brother to Syracuse.

Roman Actors from Bas-Relief, Farnese Palace

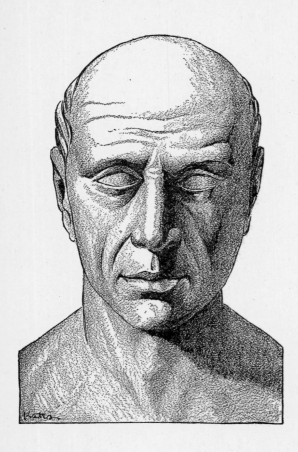

Publius Terentius Afer

("Terence")

··{ *Born, Carthage, Africa, 190 B.C.* }··
    Died, 158 B.C.

"WHILE there's life, there's hope." Probably every English speaking person has used or at least heard that expression at some time. Not one in a hundred, or even in a thousand, very likely, knows that it first saw the light of day in the works of the Roman dramatist posterity knows simply as Terence. It is only one of dozens of similar quotations so familiar as to have become proverbial all of which first were heard on the Roman stage.

The Roman comedy writer, Terence, was of African descent. He was brought to Rome as a slave by the Roman Senator, Terentius Lucanus, who gave him a good education and finally freed him. The success of his first play, staged in 166 B.C. gave him the opportunity of introduction into the most refined society in Rome. Here his engaging manners and accomplishments made him a prime favorite.

Terence's dramatic work was of two kinds: fairly close translations of the later Greek comedy writers, especially Menander; and "contaminations" which is the term used in referring to an amalgamation of all or parts of two or more Greek dramas into a Romanized whole. By some happy chance six of Terence's comedies were preserved through the Dark Ages and later were studied by some of the greatest playwrights, particularly Molière. The extant plays are: *Andria, Hecyra, Heautontimoroumenos, Eunuchus, Phormio,* and *Adelphi.* The latter play, probably a sort of rehash of both Diphilus and Menander, is best known.

Since Plautus and Terence are practically the only Roman dramatists, if one excepts the "closet" dramas of Seneca, it is natural that the work of the two should be rather critically compared. Terence is undoubtedly inferior to Plautus in comic power. The swift-moving action and vigor of Plautine comedies, too, are lacking in the plays of Terence. He is, however, more than a match for his predecessor in consistency of plot and characterization. "Plautus was the practical playwright; Terence, the elegant literary craftsman."[1] Plautus was the playwright of the masses; Terence, of the classes.

In 158 B.C. Terence departed on a trip to Greece to study the comedies of Menander, Diphilus and Apollodorus against their native background. He never returned and tradition says he was drowned.

[1] Martha Bellinger in *A Short History of the Drama.*

ADELPHI

First performed in 160 B.C. at the funeral games of Æmilius Paulus

SCENE: *A street on which front the dwellings of Micio and the betrayed sweetheart of Æschinus.*

THE farmer, Demea, has two sons. One of them, Æschinus, he gives to his bachelor brother, Micio, who lives the life of a man-about-town in the near-by city. The other son, Ctesipho, he keeps on the farm and brings up very strictly into a young manhood that is supposed to be a model of right living. Æschinus, on the other hand, under the care of his lax and pleasure-loving uncle, has acquired a reputation for wildness. In following his pleasure, he has betrayed an Athenian girl of good but impoverished family. Being kindhearted by nature and really somewhat in love with the girl, he has agreed to marry her but has not confessed his predicament to his uncle.

Meanwhile, Ctesipho, who because of his strict upbringing is all the wilder when he gets away from his father's supervision, has been captivated by the charms of a Music Girl. Æschinus aids and abets his country brother in this affair even to letting it be thought that he is the one involved. Finally he even carries off the Music Girl from her master, the Procurer, and brings her to his uncle's house where his brother may enjoy her society with less risk of discovery.

This might all have been very well had not the mother of the betrayed girl heard of it. Thinking that Æschinus means to go back on his promise to her daughter, she gets her kinsman to report the whole affair to Demea. The countryman, who has come to town to look for Ctesipho, decides that he will go to his brother's house. There he will likely find Ctesipho and at the same time will upbraid Micio for the way he is allowing Æschinus to treat his erstwhile sweetheart. It is only through most amusing subterfuges of Syrus, Micio's trusted slave, that Demea is prevented from entering the house and discovering Ctesipho with his Music Girl.

In the end, of course, Æschinus is permitted to marry, as he has promised. Demea, convinced that honey catches more flies than molasses, becomes as agreeable as his brother, Micio. On the theory that all work and no play is doubtless a mistake, he even permits Ctesipho to take his Music Girl out to the farm. And, most unbelievably, Micio is persuaded to give up his carefree bachelor life and marry the mother of Æschinus' wife. As usual in such comedies, Syrus, the trusted slave, contrives to be given his freedom together with the wherewithal to set himself up.

EVERYMAN

This play is probably the finest and best known of the morality plays of the Middle Ages that have come down to us. Consensus of critical opinion agrees that it is a translation from the Dutch made probably toward the end of the 15th century. Its popularity in England of that day is attested by the fact that it was printed four different times early in the 16th century.

THE Lord God looks down on Everyman from on high. He sees that Everyman in his seeking for riches and pleasure has forgotten God and He is much displeased. He calls His messenger, Death, and bids him take to Everyman the message that he must go on a long journey; that he must prepare to make his accounting before the Almighty God.

Everyman is loath to leave this earth. He pleads that he is not ready and offers Death a thousand pounds if Death will reprieve him. Death refuses saying that all the riches in the world might be his if he were open to such bribes. Everyman next inquires if he will be allowed to return after he has rendered his account to Almighty God. Death assures him that from the place to which he is going there is no returning. At last, however, Death consents that Everyman may try to find someone to bear him company on the journey.

Everyman first approaches Fellowship who inquires the cause of his sadness. Fellowship protests that he will do anything for Everyman even to avenging a wrong done him at the risk of his own life. When, however, Everyman invites Fellowship to join him in the journey of Death, Fellowship promptly declines and hastens away.

Everyman next bethinks himself of his kinsmen. Some one of them he reasons will make the journey with him, for blood is thicker than water. When the kinsmen find, however, that it is for the journey from which there is no returning that Everyman desires companionship, they beg to be excused. Everyman approaches his Worldly Goods with no better fortune. They assure him that they could only bring him straightway to Hell.

At last he recalls his Good Deeds. She is so weak and helpless by means of Everyman's neglect that she cannot stand. Only after Everyman is taken to Confession and does penance for his sins does Good Deeds get strength enough to accompany him. Good Deeds and Knowledge advise him to take with him on the journey Discretion, Strength, and Beauty, and, as counsellors, his Five Senses. Everyman receives the Last Sacrament and sets out on his journey with these companions. But when he actually reaches the grave, Beauty makes haste to depart and is promptly followed by Strength. At last only Knowledge and Good Deeds remain by his side. Good Deeds accompanies him to the Heavenly realm to plead his cause before his Maker, and Knowledge, remaining behind, hears the joyful songs of the angels.

from 16th Century Woodcuts

THE FARCE OF PIERRE PATHELIN

The origin of this French farce is unknown. It was played by the Fraternity of the Bazôche in Paris as early as 1480 and apparently was immensely popular. Later it served as the libretto for an opera by Bazin.

SCENE: *A French village.*

PIERRE PATHELIN, a shyster lawyer of mediaeval France, is living in dire poverty. His wife complains bitterly about their situation, particularly her lack of clothes, and taunts her husband with his failure to provide as other husbands do. Spurred to action by his wife's taunts, Pierse boasts that that very day she shall have cloth of the finest for a new frock and he some of the same for a badly needed suit of clothes. Although he has no money to pay for it, he manages to wheedle six yards of woolen cloth out of the village Draper. When, after a reasonable time, payment is not forth-

coming, the Draper goes to Pathelin's house to collect. The lawyer is discovered ill in bed and his wife declares that he has not been out of the house for weeks. In fact, the Draper is almost persuaded that he has dreamed the whole affair and returns to his shop to make sure that the cloth is really missing.

When he finds that it is without doubt entirely gone he rushes back to Pierre's house. This time Pierre pretends to be insane and overwhelms him with a torrent of words in first one and then another of the French dialects. Then he starts chasing the Draper around the room threatening both the visitor and his own wife. His wife helps on the hoax by pretending great terror, first begging the Draper to protect her and then urging him to go quickly to save his own life. She pretends that the presence of a stranger aggravates her husband's mental illness but that if left alone she can persuade him to go back to bed. At last the Draper retires in utter confusion.

Meanwhile the Draper has lost some sheep and is suing the Shepherd whom he accuses of having stolen them. The Shepherd engages Pierre Pathelin as defense lawyer. When the case comes up in court Pathelin advises his client to pretend to be an idiot and to all the judge's questions to answer simply "Baa-a."

When the Draper catches sight of Pathelin in court he promptly begins a tirade about the stolen cloth. The judge unable to bring the Draper back to the question of sheep is finally forced to acquit the Shepherd for lack of evidence. But when the lawyer, in turn, attempts to collect his fee from the Shepherd, the Shepherd simply answers "Baa-a."

Lope Felix de Vega Carpio

.·{ *Born, Madrid, Spain, 1562* }·.
   { *Died, Madrid, Spain, 1635* }

THE writer, generally referred to simply as Lope de Vega, was the greatest and most prolific dramatist of Spain's "Golden Age." He is credited with having written between 1500 and 1800 secular plays dealing with every sort of subject in addition to several hundred autos, those religious plays that resembled the English mysteries of the Middle Ages. It is said that he could write a complete play in a single day, and we may well believe it.

Born in the family of a poverty-stricken nobleman, Lope received his elementary training under the Jesuits in the Imperial College. Before he was twelve he had written two plays which, strangely enough, are among those that have come down to posterity. As a young man he served in the campaign that resulted in the destruction of the Spanish Armada. Military service, however, apparently was not permitted to interrupt the flow of de Vega's literary activity, for, according to tradition, he wrote steadily even on shipboard.

Lope was a poet of great versatility and at some time or other essayed nearly every form of writing, but it is as a dramatist that his genius stands out. His plays are remarkable for fertile imagination, skill in characterization and an always spirited dialogue. His disregard of the three unities did for Spain what Shakspere did for England . . . gave it a national theater.

Of some 2200 plays, 50 autos and 431 comedies survive; of these *The Star of Seville* is easily the best. It is probable that the autos stem from the fact that Philip II on his deathbed forbade the presentation of secular drama in Spain for an indefinite time. In addition to the autos, de Vega wrote three other types of play: (1) "dramas of the cloak and sword" whose spirited and gallant hero overcame all obstacles to win the lady of his love; (2) similar dramas of adventure dealing with historical and semi-historical personages; (3) a small group of "social" dramas portraying contemporary life.

Lope de Vega's plays brought him wealth and renown. Whenever he left his house he was followed by admiring crowds. He was frequently referred to as the "Spanish Phœnix" and "Prodigy of Nature." A couple of years after the death in 1612 of his second wife he took religious orders. At his death no vestige of his great fortune remained; only the memory of his pomp and of his generosity toward the poor. His funeral was observed like a king's with three bishops to officiate and a three-day period of mourning for the city.

THE STAR OF SEVILLE

First presented by a company headed by Cristóbal de Avendaño sometime after 1621 and probably in the first half of 1623 at the theater in Madrid.

SCENE: *The city of Seville.*

THROUGHOUT all Seville, Stella Tabera is known for her virtue and for a wondrous beauty which has earned for her the title of "Star of Seville." Her brother, Bustos, is scarcely less famed for his unyielding uprightness. Stella is looking forward to marriage with her brother's best friend, Don Sancho Ortiz, when the King of Castile makes a visit to the city. A chance glimpse of Stella inflames the royal desires and the King promptly seeks her identity.

Arias, his informant and confidant, advises the King to attain his desires by showering honors on the girl's brother. Bustos's sound common sense frustrates this scheme, and when Stella herself is approached with suggestions of a titled marriage in return for her favors, she coldly turns her back. As a final resort, Arias bribes the slave, Mathilde, to admit the King at night when Bustos is away.

Bustos's unexpected return and attack on the unknown intruder force the King to reveal his identity. When lights brought by the servants confirm the truth of his statement, he is, of course, allowed to depart unharmed but nursing a burning hatred for the man who has exposed his unkingly actions. Not daring to have Bustos killed openly on account of his high standing in Seville, His Majesty consults Arias as to whom he may find with sufficient bravery and discretion for the deed. Arias recommends Don Sancho Ortiz and so it comes about that Don Sancho on his wedding morning receives the royal command to kill his best friend, brother of the girl he loves.

Since Sancho has no choice but to accept the royal command and the royal assurance of his personal safety, he inveigles Bustos into a

quarrel and kills him, after which he promptly surrenders to the authorities. His refusal to tell the reason for his action puts the King in a dilemma. Either the royal word of honor must be broken or the King must reveal his own dastardly part in the affair. A solution seems to offer when Stella appears in the royal presence to beg that vengeance for her brother's death be put in her hands. She uses the royal permission, however, only to free Sancho, a freedom which he refuses as soon as he learns the identity of his savior.

Thus finally the King is forced to acknowledge his own responsibility and Sancho's honor is cleared. But the barrier of a brother's blood cannot be overcome nor forgotten and Stella and Sancho part forever.

Spanish Theatre

Calderon

..{ *Born, Madrid, Spain, 1600*
Died, Probably Madrid, 1681 }..

PEDRO CALDERON de la BARCA, generally referred to simply as Calderon, ranks
next to Lope de Vega in the list of Spanish
dramatists. He came of a substantial old family
and his father held a government position. His
education was secured at the Jesuit College in
Madrid, and later he studied law, though there
is no record of his having practiced before the
courts. As early as his thirteenth year he felt
the urge to write plays and created the first of
the long list which he was destined to leave for
future generations. What this play was and
whether or not it was published, the records do
not say.

Calderon was still very young when he was
commissioned by Philip IV to write a series of
plays for the royal theater in the Buen Retiro.
In 1637, possibly in recognition of this service,
the King made him a Knight of the Order of
Santiago. Later his play-writing career was
interrupted by military duty. He took part
in the campaign against the Catalan uprising
and rendered conspicuous and gallant service.
After his retirement from the army on account
of ill health he was granted a military pension.

Calderon's early plays had been of a secular
nature. After the death of his mistress in 1648,
however, his thoughts turned toward religion
and he took orders, later entering the priesthood
just as de Vega had done. Quite naturally his
later dramas are deeply religious in theme and
treatment. In fact, many commentators think
that Calderon was at his best as a writer of
"autos," those religious plays that so closely
resemble the English Mystery plays of the
Middle Ages. About 80 of these "autos" survive in addition to 120 of the regular dramas.

With Calderon the Golden Age of Spanish
drama came to a close. His thought was not
universal like that of Shakspere and Molière.
Instead it was intensely local. His characters
are less individuals in their own right than they
are personifications of certain primitive passions.
His plot motives are practically limited to three:
loyalty to the King, devotion to the church, and
the protection or assertion of one's honor
through revenge.

Calderon wrote right up to the time of his
death, apparently without any diminution of
his powers or his interest. Nor did the fact
that much of his life was spent in poor health
seem to affect the quality or quantity of his output. Probably the best known of his dramatic
works, so far as present day readers are concerned, is the secular play, *Life Is a Dream*.

LIFE IS A DREAM

Published in 1636 or 1637 before Calderon was forty. Inasmuch as plays in seventeenth century Spain were written primarily for immediate production it is probable that this play had been presented on the Madrid stage before that date.

SCENE: *The Polish frontier; Warsaw.*

THE horoscope of the infant Prince, Segismund, convinces the Polish King, Basilio, that Segismund is destined to bring dishonor on Poland and downfall to his father, Basilio. He therefore announces that Segismund has died with his mother in birth. Confined in a tower, deep in the rocky fastnesses of the frontier, Segismund grows to manhood chained like an animal to a ring in the floor, guarded under direction of Basilio's confidential general, Clotaldo.

As the play opens two strangers whose storm-frighted horses have bolted, stumble on Segismund's prison. One of them confesses in a voice all too gentle for her masculine attire that she has come from Muscovy on a matter of vengeance and Segismund, for the moment unguarded, confesses that he too, thinks often on revenge. Clotaldo's appearance is about to result in death for the newcomers when the general recognizes the stranger's sword as one he had left years before in Muscovy as pledge for favor owed. The stranger identifies herself as Rosaura, daughter of Clotaldo's quondam benefactor, and is proffered safe conduct to Warsaw.

Meanwhile the King has Segismund brought to court while in a drugged sleep, to wake to all the appurtenances of royal splendor. His tragic story is related to him, he meets his cousins, Astolfo and Estrella, and falls promptly in love with the latter. When, however, his father, the King, appears, his desire for revenge on an unnatural father is too strong and he would have attacked the King had not the guards prevented. For this action he is returned in a drugged sleep to his prison and the King prepares to carry out his plans to marry his nephew, Duke Astolfo of Muscovy, to his niece, Estrella, and turn over his Kingdom to them.

Meanwhile, back in his prison Segismund is convinced by Clotaldo that the entire day's happenings are but a dream. Clotaldo nevertheless chides him for his unprincelike lack of self-control so effectively that when later in the day he is rescued by revolting Polish troops directed to his prison by Rosaura, he treats the vanquished King with great nobility and returns to him his forfeit crown. When he discovers that Astolfo had broken his engagement to Rosaura in hopes of gaining the Polish crown through marriage to Estrella, he dissolves the new bond, returning Astolfo to Rosaura and claims Estrella for himself.

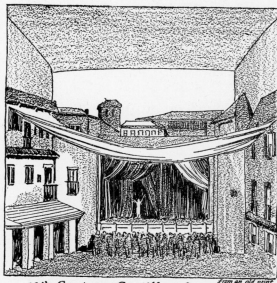

16ᵗʰ **Century Castillan Stage** *from an old print*

Bankside, London about 1600

Thomas Kyd

.·{ *Born, London, 1558* }·.
.·{ *Died, London, 1595* }·.

UNTIL the last decade of the 19th century practically nothing was known about the life of the Elizabethan dramatist, Thomas Kyd. Although his famous *Spanish Tragedy*, produced about 1587, enjoyed immense popularity on the stage all through Elizabeth's reign and through the succeeding reigns of James I and Charles I, not even his name was known in connection with it until 1773. At that time it was accidentally discovered in a treatise written by Thomas Heywood in which reference was made to the *Spanish*

Tragedy, or *Hieronimo* as it was more generally called by Kyd's contemporaries.

Thomas Kyd, we have learned, was the son of a London scrivener. What formal education he received probably was had at the Merchant Taylor's School where he acquired at least a smattering of Latin, French, Italian and Spanish. He seems to have been included in the Mermaid Tavern group although he appears not to have been the equal of most of them either in birth or in education.

About the time of the production of the *Spanish Tragedy*, or shortly after, Kyd evidently came into a fairly close association with Marlowe. From 1590 to 1593 both dramatists were in the service of the same "noble lord." This contact had unfortunate results for Kyd. Some of his papers were seized in Marlowe's rooms when the government was preparing to arrest that gentleman on a charge of heresy. On the strength of this Kyd's lodging was searched and Kyd himself imprisoned and tortured. When, after the death of Marlowe, he was released, he could never regain his former place in the world and died in poverty shortly afterwards.

The two plays on the subject of the Spanish marshal, Hieronimo, are the only dramatic outpourings of Kyd's "rampant and lurid genius."[1] The *Spanish Tragedy* had everything—ghosts, insanity, murder, suicide—to shock the sensation-loving audiences of the day. There is no doubt that the play exercised a certain amount of influence on the writings of Kyd's contemporaries. Shaksperian commentators even acknowledge that famous playwright's indebtedness to Kyd's "tragedy of blood" for some of the mechanism of *Hamlet*.

For a long time *The Spanish Tragedy* was better known than any other English play in Germany where it was acted at Frankfurt in 1601. It was equally popular in Holland and exercised a powerful influence on Dutch literature. It may be that Kyd's early death cut off the flowering of genius; or it may be that the two bloody dramas that have come down to us were in reality the only plays he had in his system.

[1] Martha Bellinger in *A Short History of the Drama*.

THE SPANISH TRAGEDY

Produced in London between 1585 and 1589, probably about 1587.
SCENE: *Feudal Spain.*

ANDREA, a Spanish courtier, has been killed in battle by Balthazar, Prince of Portugal. During his lifetime he was lover of Bel-Imperia, daughter of the Duke of Castile. Now when Andrea's ghost appears before Pluto to be apportioned its proper place in the world of shadows, Pluto permits the ghost, accompanied by the spirit of Revenge, to return to earth to see vengeance wreaked on his slayer.

Andrea's slayer falls prisoner to Lorenzo, Bel-Imperia's brother and to Horatio, son of Hieronimo, marshal of Spain. The King awards the ransom to Horatio and the custody of the royal prisoner to Lorenzo. In the Duke's household, Balthazar inevitably falls in love with Bel-Imperia, and the King conceives the idea that a marriage between these two would unite the kingdoms of Spain and Portugal more firmly than a dozen wars.

Bel-Imperia, however, has secretly taken Horatio for her lover because he was Andrea's friend and had given Andrea's body burial rites. Lorenzo, keen to forward Balthazar's suit, bribes Bel-Imperia's servant to betray her meeting with Horatio. Lorenzo and Balthazar with their servants hang Horatio and imprison Bel-Imperia so that she cannot spread the truth.

Hieronimo goes raving mad when he finds his son's body, but not too mad to plan a crafty revenge. Gossip begins to spread as to Lorenzo's part in Horatio's death. Lorenzo hires one servant to kill the other and then permits the first servant to be hanged for his crime. Thus he thinks to get rid of all witnesses. But a letter recounting the details of the slaying is found on the servant's body and brought to Hieronimo.

When, with many plausible speeches, Bel-Imperia is released for the royal betrothal ceremonies, Hieronimo manages speech with her long enough to plan for their double revenge. He arranges that a play of which he is the author shall be acted for the entertainment of the royal guests with Lorenzo, Balthazar, Bel-Imperia and himself as actors. During the course of the performance Hieronimo fatally stabs Lorenzo and Bel-Imperia kills Balthazar and herself. Before he attempts to hang himself, Hieronimo explains to his audience that the deeds of blood are real, not sham, and the reason for them. The party rushes down from the royal box to prevent his self-destruction before they can learn the names of his fellow conspirators. During the confusion Hieronimo finds an opportunity to stab the Duke of Castile and himself. Thus the ghost of Andrea receives full satisfaction for Andrea's untimely death.

From Woodcut of 1615, illustrating scene of Horatio's murder

Birthplace of MARLOWE

Christopher Marlowe

..{ *Born, Canterbury, England, 1564* }..
{ *Died, Deptford, England, 1593* }

THERE can be no question of the genius of Christopher Marlowe, nor of the far-reaching effect of his work on English drama. He dared disregard the classical unities in favor of a natural unity which comes from centering the action around one great character or great passion. He created an English drama in place of a slavish imitation of Greek and Latin dramas. He was, perhaps, the pioneer who blazed a trail for that still greater English dramatist born the same year, William Shakspere.

Christopher Marlowe was the son of a shoemaker. He studied at Corpus Christi College, Cambridge, where he received his bachelor's degree in 1583. Before he received his master's degree in 1587, his greatest tragic drama had been presented on the stage. Before he finished college he had also done at least part of the work of translating Ovid's *Amores* into English verse.

After leaving college he went up to London where he gained immediate fame as a poet and dramatist writing for the Admiral's company. He numbered among his friends the literary lights of the day, including Kyd, Nash, Greene, Sir Walter Raleigh and probably Shakspere. This period of his life was characterized mainly by a revolt against conventional morality and established religion. His career came to an untimely end in a tavern brawl or over a love affair, at a time when he was about to be arrested on a charge of heresy.

In his few brief years of maturity he had accomplished more than many men do in a lifetime, and he left a lasting impress on dramatic history. His *Jew of Malta* was performed 38 times in four years, a record for those days. This same drama finds an echo a few years later in *The Merchant of Venice*. His *Dr. Faustus* is the first dramatic treatment of the *Faust* legend, later made famous by the German Goethe. His most successful attempt at historical drama is *Edward II*. His beautiful poem, *Hero and Leander* was incomplete at his death as was also a tragedy on the subject of Queen Dido.

Marlowe followed the Italian Machiavelli in admiration for mental and spiritual freedom. He tried to show the inner spiritual struggle in his plays; "he made tragedy a matter of character, not of caste." In addition, he greatly improved the blank verse that in his time was the recognized vehicle of tragic drama. But he had one important weakness: he lacked the ability to portray women and none of his plays treats of the subject of love.

Swinburne's characterization of Marlowe is most revealing: "He came to London to seek his fortune . . . a boy in years, a man in genius, a god in ambition. Who knows to what heights he might have risen but for his untimely end?"[1]

[1]Quoted in Martha Bellinger's *A Short History of the Drama.*

TAMBURLAINE

Probably produced in London early in the year 1587.

SCENE: *Asia Minor and Africa.*

THE Scythian Shepherd, Tamburlaine, moved by an ambition far beyond the circumstances of his humble birth, has made himself leader of a gang of brigands that prey successfully on the rich merchant trains that cross Persia. In one of their raids the brigands capture the party escorting Zenocrate, daughter of the Sultan of Egypt, to her nuptials with the King of Arabia. Tamburlaine promptly falls in love with her and resolves, whether she will or no, to make her his empress when that happy time shall come.

Meanwhile, Mycetes, the not too bright King of Persia, has heard that Tamburlaine might even have designs on the throne of Persia. He therefore sends one of his lords, Theridamas, with a thousand horsemen to take Tamburlaine prisoner. Such is the Scythian's eloquence, however, that Theridamas and his cavalry join Tamburlaine's ranks. Hearing this, Mycetes's brother, Cosroe, decides that the help of so powerful a man as Tamburlaine might make his own chances of seizing his brother's crown more sure. Accordingly he promises Tamburlaine preferment if he will help to unseat Mycetes. Tamburlaine and his followers do so, then turn on Cosroe and dispatch him, taking Persia for themselves.

By this time Zenocrate is as much in love with Tamburlaine as he with her. The Persian crown, alone, he decides, is all too little to offer her great beauty. His insatiable ambition impels him next to try his fortunes against the all-powerful Bajazeth, emperor of Turkey. After this conquest Tamburlaine is drunk with success. It becomes his custom on the first day of a seige to have his camp and all his accoutrements in purest white as an indication prompt surrender will save all bloodshed. Failing to receive the city's submission, the second day sees Tamburlaine's camp decked out in crimson as a sign that the resisting forces will be put to the sword. The third day all is deepest black spelling death for every living being in the hapless city.

In spite of Zenocrate's pleas, Tamburlaine now marches against her native Egypt, which her father, the Sultan, and her former betrothed of Arabia, prepare to defend. The Arabian is killed, but, true to his promise, Tamburlaine spares the Sultan and makes him one of his tributary kings. With such a valiant start toward conquering the known world Tamburlaine feels that his crown is now worth Zenocrate's acceptance and the play closes with the wedding rites.

Part II of *Tamburlaine*, evidently written at a later date due to immense popularity of Part I, details Tamburlaine's subsequent victories and inglorious death from illness.

TAMBURLAINE, *from a 16th Century Woodcut*

William Shakspere

..{ *Born, Stratford-on-Avon, 1564* }..
{ *Died, Stratford, 1616* }

TRADITION says that this greatest of English-speaking playwrights made his first
contact with the theater as a sort of handy man
of all work. One of his tasks, according to
legend, was, with the assistance of several boy
helpers, to hold the horses of the wealthy
patrons who attended the theater.

It is supposed that he left his family about
four years after his marriage to Anne Hatha-
way at the age of eighteen, and came up to
London to seek to better the family fortunes.
London had grown prosperous under the reign
of Elizabeth and at this time the group of writers
frequently spoken of as the "University Wits"

were in possession of the stage so far as the
writing of plays was concerned. But somewhere, somehow, during those early years in
London, Shakspere gained a foothold, first
probably as an actor and then perhaps as an
adaptor and hack writer.

By the early 1590's Shakspere was firmly
established in the theater. In 1599 the family
was granted a coat of arms and thereafter the
playwright was entitled to sign himself,
"William Shakspere, Gent." At the same time
his financial status was improving. He bought a
large house in Stratford and frequently after
that acquired other property both in Stratford
and London.

It has been customary among Shaksperean
Commentators to divide his dramatic work into
four periods: (1) the experimental period ending
about 1593 and including among other plays,
Love's Labour's Lost, Two Gentlemen of Verona,
and *A Comedy of Errors;* (2) the period in which he
became definitely established ending about 1601,
and marked especially by the production of
some of his best-known romantic comedies,
notably *The Merchant of Venice* and, according to
some commentators, *A Midsummer Night's Dream.*
(William Winter,[1] the noted Shaksperean expert, however, claims that this latter play was
first exhibited at the Globe Theater in 1592
which would link it definitely with the first
period.) (3) the period covered by the first ten
years of the 17th century and given over largely
to somber tragedy such as *King Lear, Hamlet,
Othello,* and *Macbeth;* (4) the period from 1610 to
the playwright's death, notable for a ripening
and enrichment of the poet's powers that
flowered in the grave, serene romances of *A
Winter's Tale,* and *The Tempest.*

Not a single original Shaksperean manuscript
has survived, due partly perhaps to the fact
that they were written, many of them hastily,
strictly for stage performance. Practically all
of Shakspere's plots were borrowed. So original
was his treatment, however, and so remarkable
his command of language, that in the process of
adaptation the borrowed plots became as truly
his own as though they had been original
products of his imagination. They have rightfully brought him a place second to none in the
records of posterity.

[1]In his *Shakspere on the Stage.*

A MIDSUMMER NIGHT'S DREAM

According to the Shaksperean expert, William Winter, this play was performed at the Globe Theater in 1592. The Encyclopedia Britannica gives the production date as 1595-6.

SCENE: *Athens and a near-by forest.*

IN ANCIENT Athens there was a law providing that if a daughter refused to marry the man of her father's choice, she could be sentenced to death. This law the stern Egeus invoked against the beautiful Hermia because she preferred her true love, Lysander, to Demetrius, the suitor favored by her father. Her excuse was that her best friend, Helena, was in love with Demetrius and that he had formerly professed his love for her.

To escape death, Hermia had agreed to meet Lysander in the wood, whence they would repair to Lysander's aunt's outside the city and there be married. Foolishly Hermia confided her plans to Helena, and Helena out of spite told Demetrius.

Now the wood where they were to meet was the haunt of Oberon and Titania, king and queen of the fairies. Just now this royal couple was at odds because Titania refused to give a little changeling boy she had adopted, to Oberon for a page. Oberon bade the mischievous Puck to bring him a certain love charm so potent that sprinkled in the eyes of a sleeper it would cause him (or her) on awakening to fall desperately in love with the first person seen. While Puck was gone to fetch it, Oberon beheld the plight of the lovesick Helena who had followed Demetrius into the wood. On Puck's return, he bade him seek out "the youth in Athenian clothes" and use the charm on him when he slept being sure that Helena was near when he awoke.

Meanwhile Oberon visited Titania's bower and used the love charm to such good effect that Titania fell in love with a clown wearing an ass head. Thereupon Oberon's taunts prevailed upon her to give up the changeling boy and the couple were reconciled.

They promptly discovered that Puck's ministrations had not turned out so fortunately. Through mistaken identity he had placed the love charm in Lysander's eyes. Lysander, being awakened by Helena who was hunting for Demetrius, began at once to profess violent love for her. Oberon, however, by using the antidote in Lysander's eyes when he again slept, restored his love for Hermia. At the same time he used the love charm in Demetrius's eyes as originally planned. About this time Egeus came hunting his daughter. When he discovered that Demetrius no longer wanted to marry her he gave his consent for her marriage with Lysander and both couples decided that their amazing experiences had been only a "Midsummer Night's Dream."

Puck   *Bottom*

ROMEO AND JULIET

According to most authorities this play from Shakspere's second period was produced in
1594 or 1595.

SCENE: *Verona; Mantua.*

THE Montagues and Capulets were the two richest and most powerful families in Verona. There existed between them an enmity so deep that it included even their most distant kin. Romeo, the son of Lord Montague, fancied himself deeply in love with the beautiful but scornful Rosaline. In order to be near her, he had the audacity to go masked to a large ball given by Lord Capulet, to which all the important citizens of Verona had been invited excepting only the Montagues. Scarcely had he arrived than he saw a girl of such transcendent loveliness that Rosaline was completely forgotten and his only thought was to learn the unknown lady's identity. By the time he discovered that his ideal was Juliet, the only daughter of Lord Capulet, he was hopelessly and irretrievably in love.

Later the same night Romeo returned to the Capulet orchard just to be near his beloved, little knowing that Juliet had been as deeply smitten as he. As he lurked there in the shadows watching, Juliet, sleepless with the wonder and the hopelessness of her new-found love, stepped out onto her balcony and avowed her love to the stars. At this, scarcely able to credit his good fortune, Romeo stepped forth and claimed her. The next day he arranged with a Friar friend in a near-by monastery to marry them. After Juliet had returned to her home, Romeo met the Capulet, Tybalt, on the street and was forced into a quarrel which resulted in Tybalt's death and Romeo's banishment.

The Friar advised him to live quietly in Mantua until the marriage could be announced and perhaps put an end to the long-standing feud. All might have been well, had not Lord Capulet suddenly insisted that Juliet marry the rich and noble Paris. In despair she consulted the Friar and received from him a potion that would enable her to feign death for forty-two hours. On the eve of her marriage she drank this potion and with due ceremony was laid away in the family tomb from which the Friar had promised Romeo should rescue her.

But before the Friar's messenger explaining the real truth arrived rumor had acquainted Romeo with the news of his beloved's death. Buying a deadly poison, he set out at once to die by Juliet's side. When Juliet awakened and saw the poison cup and Romeo's dead body, she realized at once what had happened. Seizing his dagger she promptly ended her own life. Thus at last, grief for the needless sacrifice of their only children ended the long-standing feud between the houses of Montague and Capulet.

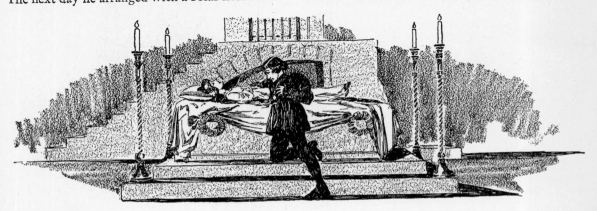

THE MERCHANT OF VENICE

Produced between the autumns of 1596 and 1597 (Encyclopedia Britannica).

SCENE: *Partly at Venice; partly at Belmont, Portia's home.*

SHYLOCK, a Jewish moneylender of Venice, was in great disfavor with the Christians on account of the high interest rates he demanded. Antonio, on the other hand, a fine, upstanding young Christian merchant, had incurred the enmity of Shylock by lending money gratis.

Antonio's best friend, Bassanio, wishing to court the fair and wealthy Portia, begged Antonio for a loan of three thousand ducats. Since, at the moment, all Antonio's cash was invested in merchandise three ships were bringing, he arranged to borrow the money from Shylock, in jest signing a bond that would give the Jew a pound of flesh should Antonio default.

Bassanio's courtship was successful as was that of his man, Gratiano, for the hand of Nerissa, Portia's lady-in-waiting. The two couples were married forthwith and both ladies made their husbands presents of rings which the gentlemen swore to keep always. Scarcely was the ceremony over when Bassanio received a note telling him that Antonio's ships were lost and his life forfeit. Bassanio hurriedly returned to Venice to offer Shylock many times his three thousand ducats, only to meet refusal.

At the trial an unknown young lawyer represented Antonio. The court perforce awarded Shylock his pound of flesh but as he was about to take it, the stranger halted him with the warning that if he shed one drop of Christian blood his fortune would by the laws of Venice be confiscated to the state. Bitterly disappointed, Shylock was about to accept the money Bassanio offered when the lawyer again stopped him with the declaration that since he was guilty of conspiracy against the life of a Christian, his own life and property were already forfeit to the state.

To emphasize the difference in the Christian attitude, however, the court forgave the old man. Antonio, likewise, generously returned the half of Shylock's property that had been forfeit to him as the injured party, on condition that Shylock leave it to the daughter he had disinherited for marrying a Christian.

Since lawyer and clerk would take no other fee than the rings Bassanio and Gratiano wore, these gentlemen with much misgiving surrendered their wives' gifts, and, with Antonio, set out for Portia's home. Immediately on their arrival Portia and Nerissa missed the rings and pretended to disbelieve their husbands' explanations. At last they gave their husbands new rings which they bade them guard more carefully. By these rings Portia was revealed as lawyer and Nerissa as clerk. Meanwhile Antonio's ships arrived safely and all ended happily.

HAMLET

According to the Encyclopedia Britannica, Hamlet was first presented on the London stage between the autumn of 1600 and that of 1601.

SCENE: *The royal court of Denmark.*

SCARCE two months after the death of Hamlet, King of Denmark, his widow, Gertrude, married his brother, Claudius. This circumstance caused the young Prince Hamlet to wonder if his uncle had not, indeed, murdered the king. Between grief for his father and worry as to his mother's share in the crime, Hamlet was on the verge of losing his reason. While he was in this melancholy mood, his father's ghost appeared to him, described the manner of his murder by Claudius and begged Hamlet to avenge him.

Hamlet decided that his life would be safer while he made up his mind what to do, if he pretended insanity. At length, through his uncle's reaction to a play that reënacted the

murder of his father, Hamlet satisfied himself that the ghost spoke truly. Claudius, however, became suspicious of Hamlet and bade the queen talk to him. Lest she should not report the conversation truly, the King directed the crafty old diplomat, Polonius, to secrete himself in the hangings of the queen's room. During their conversation Hamlet discovered the presence of a third party and, believing it to be the King, stabbed the intruder, only to discover that he had killed the father of his beloved Ophelia.

After this, on pretense that it was for Hamlet's safety, the King deported the young Prince to England with private instructions that he should be killed on landing there. Hamlet, however, fell captive to a pirate ship whose crew set him again ashore in Denmark. He arrived at the court just as funeral ceremonies were being held for Ophelia whose reason had been unsettled by her father's death at the hands of her lover.

Since his first plan for getting rid of Hamlet had failed, the King now arranged a fencing match between Hamlet and Ophelia's brother, Laertes. He persuaded Laertes to use an unguarded sword whose point had been dipped in poison. Hamlet, who had used a foil, was angered when Laertes' weapon pricked his skin, and, seizing the same sword, wounded Laertes.

Realizing that he was about to die, Laertes confessed and warned Hamlet that he had but half an hour to live. Meanwhile the queen had drunk a bowl of poisoned wine prepared by the King for Hamlet. Shrieking that she was poisoned she fell dead. Seizing the sword on whose tip a little poison still remained, Hamlet dispatched the King before he himself fell dead. Thus was the murder of his father avenged.

OTHELLO

Produced in 1604–05.

Scene: *Venice; the Island of Cyprus.*

DESDEMONA, only daughter of the Venetian Senator, Brabantio, chose from among her many suitors, Othello, the black Moor, because of his nobility of soul and his eloquence in describing his adventures. Now Othello was foremost general of the State of Venice and at this time sorely needed to repulse the Turkish forces who were even then sailing against the Island of Cyrpus. Nevertheless, the Venetian Senate listened fairly to the charges of Brabantio that Othello had successfully wooed his daughter only through the use of sorcery. Othello's defense was so straightforward and so eloquent that they rightfully absolved him of any guilt, whereupon he and his bride set sail for Cyprus.

Meanwhile storms dispersed the Turkish fleet so that the troops on the island had no occupation except that of enjoying themselves. During his courtship Othello had used Cassio, a good-looking young Italian whom he loved and trusted, to further his suit with Desdemona. Now, when a lieutenancy was left vacant, he promoted Cassio to the post instead of the older Iago who had expected the preferment.

The jealous Iago at once began to plot how through a drunken brawl he might discredit Cassio with his general and further how he might arouse Othello's jealousy of his wife and thus encompass the destruction of Othello, Cassio and Desdemona at one and the same time. He began by dropping hints as to the unwarranted friendliness between Desdemona and Cassio. When Othello disdained to suspect either his wife or his friend, Iago, through the theft of a handkerchief which Othello had given his wife, produced what appeared to be proof of Desdemona's infidelity. This latter scheme was so thoroughly successful that Othello, believing the worst of his wife, smothered her beneath the bed clothes. Meanwhile

the hireling, engaged by Iago to kill Cassio, merely wounded his victim but was himself killed. Letters found upon his body proved beyond a doubt Iago's dastardly plot and Cassio's innocence.

Thus at the very moment when Othello was releasing Desdemona's lifeless body, Cassio entered to ask wherein he had offended his general. The letters and Cassio's story revealed at once the whole conspiracy and in an agony of remorse for the beloved wife whose life he had unjustly taken, Othello took his own life there beside her. Iago's treason, however, did not go unpunished for he was put to death with torture.

KING LEAR

Produced between autumn 1605 and autumn 1606.

SCENE: *Britain.*

KING LEAR of Britain was old and wearied of the responsibilities of power. After much thought he decided that he would divide his kingdom among his three daughters according as they professed love for their father. He believed that, of course, his youngest and favorite daughter, Cordelia, would merit the largest share. Goneril and Regan, his two married daughters, were extravagant in their protestations of love, but Cordelia, disgusted with her sisters' insincerity, answered simply that she loved her father as much as was her duty, no more and no less. The enraged Lear thereupon divided his kingdom between his two

Edwin Forrest as King Lear

older daughters, arranging to spend alternate months with each of them.

Prior to this there had been two ardent suitors for Cordelia's hand . . . the Duke of Burgundy and the King of France. Now, the Duke of Burgundy suddenly found his affection miraculously cooled. The King of France, however, appreciated Cordelia's true worth and took her back to France to reign as his queen.

No sooner was his youngest daughter gone than Lear began to learn to his sorrow how false had been her sisters' protestations of love. In less than a month he was driven out of the homes of both to wander unattended and half-crazed in the fields. Cordelia, hearing of her father's plight, begged from her husband an armed force and returned to Britain to reinstate Lear on his throne.

Meanwhile, Regan and Goneril, unfaithful to their husbands, were both enamored of the evil Duke of Gloucester whom they placed at the head of an army to defend their kingdom against Cordelia's troops. Just at this time Regan's husband conveniently died and she promptly announced her forthcoming marriage to Gloucester. This so enraged Goneril that she poisoned her sister. Her husband, however, who had been no party to any of her disgraceful behavior, discovered her latest crime and had her thrown into prison where she ended her own life.

The Duke of Gloucester, meanwhile, was victorious over Cordelia's forces and threw her into prison where she likewise died. Later the evil Duke was in turn killed in single combat by the brother he had cheated out of his inheritance. During all this Lear had finally died of grief and old age and had left no heirs. Goneril's husband, therefore, ascended the throne and peace settled once more over Britain.

MACBETH

This tragedy is believed first to have been presented on the London stage between the autumn of 1605 and that of 1606.

SCENE: *Scotland; England.*

DURING the reign of Duncan the Meek, there lived in Scotland a great lord and brave general, Macbeth, Thane of Glamis. As he and Banquo, a friend and brother general, were returning victorious from war, they were met upon the heath by three witches who, in addition to his rightful title, saluted Macbeth as Thane of Cawdor and King of Scotland. Turning to Banquo, they saluted him as father of a line of Scottish kings to come.

Arrived at his castle Macbeth discovered that he had, indeed, been made Thane of Cawdor by a grateful sovereign. At once Macbeth began to think enviously of the crown of Scotland. Led on by the iron-willed Lady Macbeth, he murdered King Duncan who was his guest at the castle, contriving to throw the blame on two grooms of the bedchamber. When, following the murder, Duncan's young sons fled the country, Macbeth as next of kin ascended the throne.

Scarcely had he acceded to the kingship before he and his lady began to worry about the prophecy that Banquo's children should succeed him. Inviting all his nobles to a huge banquet, he arranged to have Banquo and his son, Fleance, waylaid and slain. Fleance escaped, but Banquo fell and as the guests at the palace were about to seat themselves, the ghost of the slain man, visible only to Macbeth, took his place at the table. This so unnerved Macbeth that his queen dismissed the gathering on the plea that her husband was ill.

Wishing to know the worst, Macbeth again sought out the witches. They assured him his throne was safe until "Birnam wood to high Dunsinane Hill shall move;" likewise, that "no man born of woman" should do him bodily harm. Fortified in spirit Macbeth returned and shut himself within the palace to await the attack of the great forces gathered against him under Malcolm, Duncan's elder son.

By this time the many murders were preying so heavily on the queen's mind that she fell ill and died, leaving Macbeth without counsel or comfort. As the attacking army approached, a member of the watch came running to Macbeth in great alarm to report that far-off Birnam wood seemed to be moving nearer. Although it was only the attackers carrying branches as camouflage, Macbeth realized its significance. With the valor of despair he rushed forth believing that his life, at least, was safe. But the Thane Macduff, "taken untimely from his mother's womb," fulfilled the final prophecy, avenging his murdered wife and sons. Thus ended the bloody tale of Macbeth's unholy ambition, and Malcolm, the rightful king, ascended the Scottish throne.

"I have no words, my voice is in my sword"

THE TEMPEST

Produced between the autumns of 1611 and 1612.

Scene: *An island in the sea near Italy.*

PROSPERO and his beautiful daughter, Miranda, were the only inhabitants of a lonely island in the sea. Formerly this island had been the home of the wicked witch, Sycorax, and her ugly, misshapen son, Caliban. Through the magic arts to whose study Prospero devoted most of his time, he was able to free the good spirits that Sycorax had imprisoned in the trees. To one of these, the mischievous but kindly sprite, Ariel, he had with the promise of eventual freedom given the business of seeing that the slave, Caliban, performed his allotted tasks. Thus with only these two to serve them, Prospero and Miranda had lived on the island since Miranda was so young that she had scarce any recollection of another sort of life.

Realizing that Miranda was growing up, Prospero decided it was time that she knew her real identity. Moreover, he felt that he must provide a suitable husband for her. So he explained at great length how he himself had formerly been Duke of Milan; how he had been so engrossed in his studies that he had given over affairs of state to his younger brother; how this younger brother had conspired with the the King of Naples to seize the dukedom; and finally, how, marooned in an open boat upon the sea, the erstwhile duke and his three-year-old daughter had drifted to this island.

Now through his magical powers he pointed out to Miranda a fine boat being driven toward their island by so severe a storm that it seemed all on board must surely perish. On the boat, he told her, were her traitor uncle and the King of Naples. He did not, however, mention that Ferdinand, the comely son of the Neapolitan King was also a passenger; nor that Ferdinand, presently thinking to save himself, would jump overboard and be carried by the waves to the island. Instead, he put Miranda into a sound sleep, and when she awoke it was to behold Ferdinand guided to that part of the beach through Ariel's efficient ministrations.

Naturally the young people fell promptly in love. Meanwhile the storm had cast Miranda's uncle and the King of Naples ashore on another part of the beach and there their terror enhanced by certain pranks of Ariel's brought about in their hearts a sincere repentance. Thereupon, Ariel led them to Prospero whose forgiveness they begged. When the King had pronounced his blessing on the love of Ferdinand and Miranda, the whole company embarked on the ship which Prospero's magic had after all brought safe into harbor.

Jean Baptiste Poquelin De Molière

..{ *Born, Paris, France, 1622* }..
Died, Paris, 1675

" 'TIS a mighty stroke at any vice to make it the laughing stock of everybody; for men will easily suffer reproof; but they can by no means endure mockery. They will consent to be wicked but not ridiculous."[1]

These are the words of the man who is rated by most critics as the greatest comic dramatist of all times and considered worthy to stand with Sophocles and Shakspere. They were written in defense of the play, *Tartuffe*, ranked as his most outstanding and most representative play. For in the 17th century, as in ours, powerful cliques attempted to censor every play that did not happen to coincide with their own views or selfish interests. We can realize the bitterness of the campaign against *Tartuffe* from the fact that it was not finally licensed for public performance until more than three years after its first performance before Louis XIV.

"Molière" was in reality only the stage name assumed when, as a young man, the embryo genius joined a group of strolling players. So famous did he make it, that few of us today recognize the family surname "Poquelin." Molière's father was a prosperous tradesman, upholsterer to the King by appointment. Since this was an hereditary honor, the son shrewdly made use of it to establish and strengthen himself in the King's favor, when, after twelve years in the provinces, he returned to Paris.

These twelve years of trouping and training not only made of Molière a comedian of unsurpassed ability; they also gave him that insight into life and character that were to make his later comedies outstanding, perhaps, for all time. He was 36 when he returned to establish himself in Paris. At 40, successful in his profession and in prosperous circumstances, he married the twenty year old sister of Madeleine Bejart, his leading lady. Owing probably to the disparity in their ages and to his own jealousy, the marriage was not wholly a success. This with the death of a favorite son, and the constantly increasing attacks of the various groups who had found themselves and their pretensions the butt of Molière's biting satire, made his later years unhappy. He still wrote and acted his own plays, however, and it was in the midst of a stage performance that he burst a blood vessel in a fit of coughing and died almost at once.

Fit to be ranked with his masterpiece, *Tartuffe*, are *Don Juan*, *The Misanthrope*, and *The Learned Ladies*, while a host of lesser comedies are still read and revived on the French stage to this day.

[1] Molière in his preface to the first edition of *Tartuffe*.

TARTUFFE or THE HYPOCRITE

First three acts produced at Versailles, May 12, 1664. Finished production in present form, February 5, 1669, in Paris.

SCENE: *Paris.*

ORGON, a well-to-do Parisian householder, has been so deceived by the hypocritical cant of a poor beggar named Tartuffe, that he has made the latter an honored guest in his household. In no time at all Tartuffe has made himself practically master of the house and the doings of its occupants. Orgon, far from being incensed, ascribes this to Tartuffe's unselfish interest in his, Orgon's, welfare. He is on the point, in fact, of repudiating his promise to young Valère that he shall marry Orgon's daughter, Marianne, in order that her hand and her dower may go to Tartuffe and attach him permanently to the family.

In an effort to save her step-daughter's romance, Elmire, Orgon's wife, meets Tartuffe to beg him to refuse such a marriage. Tartuffe,

believing they are alone, proposes a clandestine love affair to the wife of his benefactor. Orgon's son, Damis, steps forth from a closet where he has been hiding during the interview, just as Orgon enters the room. Damis denounces Tartuffe for the scoundrel he is. Orgon, however, refuses to believe either his son, Damis, or his wife, Elmire. Instead he disinherits his son and drives him from the house. Not satisfied with these amends to Tartuffe's wounded "innocence," he forthwith makes Tartuffe a deed of gift for the house itself. He declares, moreover, that the marriage with Marianne shall take place at once.

Elmire, in desperation, asks Orgon if he should behold Tartuffe's treachery with his own eyes and hear it with his own ears if he would believe. Upon Orgon's incredulous assent, she conceals him under the table and leads Tartuffe on to a second avowal of illicit love. When Orgon in righteous indignation orders him from the house, Tartuffe reminds his benefactor that the house is no longer his. In fact, the bailiff presently arrives to oust Orgon and his family. At the same time Valère comes with word that Tartuffe has reported Orgon to the King for harboring property belonging to a political fugitive and that even now Tartuffe and an officer are on their way to arrest him.

As Orgon is about to flee in Valère's carriage, Tartuffe and the officer arrive. The hypocrite has at last overplayed his hand, however. Upon his appearance before the King, His Majesty had recognized him as a criminal with a long record and many aliases. So now Tartuffe is arrested in Orgon's stead. His Majesty graciously forgives Orgon his indiscretion on account of his recent conspicuous bravery in military service. His property is restored to him and Valère and Marianne are free to marry with Orgon's blessing.

DON JUAN or THE STONE GUEST

Produced at the Palais Royal, Paris, February 15, 1665, with Molière playing the part of Sganarelle.

SCENE: *Sicily.*

DON JUAN is a graceless brigand of hearts, the despair of his servant, Sganarelle, and of his upright old father who must repeatedly rescue him from some scrape. Don Juan's favorite method of procedure is to go through a secret mock marriage. This satisfies the girl yet leaves him legally free when he tires of her charms. His latest conquest is the beautiful Elvire whom he has enticed from a convent to "marry" him.

Now, in spite of Sganarelle's protests and warnings of Heaven's wrath, Don Juan has abandoned Elvire and is plotting to carry off the fiancée of a friend. With this purpose master and man embark in a small boat on the lake where the engaged couple have planned to go sailing. During a sudden squall, the small boat is overturned and both would have perished except for their timely rescue by a peasant. Scarcely are Don Juan's fancy clothes dried, before he is again at his love making . . . this time proposing marriage to each of two peasant girls who fall to quarreling as to which of them will be favored. Sganarelle, sotto voce, informs them that his master will actually marry neither one.

At this point word reaches Don Juan that Elvire's brothers have sworn to kill him. Disguised beyond recognition, master and man set out to return to the city. On the way Don Juan rescues a stranger from robbers only to discover that he has saved the life of one of Elvire's brothers. Because of his vow of gratitude before he learns Don Juan's identity the stranger spares Don Juan's life for the nonce.

Once more on their way, Don Juan and Sganarelle come to the tomb of the Commandant who had been a recent victim. As a joke, Don Juan insists that Sganarelle must invite the statue to dinner. Sganarelle is frankly frightened and Don Juan is somewhat taken aback

when the statue nods its acceptance and Sganarelle is terrified when at the dinner hour it actually appears. It is, the servant points out, a sign of Heaven's just wrath.

Heaven's wrath, however, does not concern Don Juan. It is his earthly troubles that decide him to pretend a conversion to religion. This hypocrisy proves the last straw for a long suffering Heaven. In the midst of his hypocritical cantings there is a great peal of thunder and Don Juan is swallowed up in a flaming abyss, leaving Sganarelle to remark:

"By his death everyone gets satisfaction. Heaven offended, laws violated, girls led astray, families dishonored, relatives outraged, wives ruined, husbands driven to despair, they all are satisfied. I am the only unlucky one. My wages, my wages, my wages!"

THE LEARNED LADIES

Produced March 11, 1672, at the Palais Royal in Paris with Molière playing the part of Chrysale.

SCENE: *A room in Chrysale's house.*

CHRYSALE, a citizen of Paris, deludes himself into believing that because he shouts his orders in a loud voice, he is master of his household. In reality, however, his wife, Philaminte, rules both husband and children. Her great hobby is the pretense of a profound interest in learning, a hobby which is shared by her favorite elder daughter, Armande. The younger daughter, Henriette, openly acknowledges her lack of interest in poetry, either that of Trissotin, a would-be wit who frequents the house, or of his Greek and Latin predecessors. She confesses that she is in love with young Clitandre and wants to marry him.

This confession arouses Armande's jealousy, for Clitandre was formerly her admirer and she wishes to keep him dangling. When she re

ports Henriette's conversation to her mother, that amiable lady promptly announces that she will settle matters by marrying Henriette to M. Trissotin. Her decision is unaffected by a subsequent revelation through a literary rival that Trissotin is interested only in Henriette's dower.

Meanwhile Clitandre tries to enlist supporters for his cause. He approaches Henriette's Aunt Bèlise, but that lady is useless since she insists on believing that all men are actually in love with her no matter what they may say. Chrysale's brother, Ariste, however, favors young Clitandre and pleads his cause so successfully that Chrysale declares himself in favor of an immediate wedding. Philaminte forestalls any action on her husband's part by announcing her own plans for an immediate marriage between Henriette and Trissotin. Ariste counters by encouraging his brother through taunts to send for the notary and proceed with plans for the marriage of Henriette and Clitandre.

Philaminte likewise summons the notary and when that gentleman arrives he is met with two contrary sets of instructions for drawing up the marriage contract. When it looks as though Philaminte is about to win the day, Ariste comes forward with two letters, one announcing a heavy judgment against Philaminte in a lawsuit, the other, the complete loss of Chrysale's fortune. Trissotin's ardor is promptly cooled and he retires with the excuse that he does not wish an unwilling bride.

Philaminte is about to accept the proffer of Clitandre's small fortune but Henriette refuses to go to the man she loves as a dowerless bride. This new impasse is broken by Ariste's confession that the letters were only a pretense to save Henriette. With surprising adaptability Philaminte begins gloating over the disappointment Trissotin will feel when he hears of the magnificent wedding and learns the real truth.

LE MISANTHROPE

Produced in Paris, June 4, 1666, with Molière in the part of Alceste.

SCENE: *Contemporary Paris.*

ALCESTE is one of those candid souls who believe that the truth should be spoken in season and out. He will make no concessions to ordinary courtesy and denounces the insincerities of contemporary society upon every possible occasion. His friend, Philinte, tries to make him see that honesty does not require him to go out of his way to offend and hurt people. He even points out that a few well-spoken words in the right place might go far toward bringing a favorable decision in the lawsuit Alceste has pending in the courts. To this Alceste has but one answer. If his suit cannot win through its own merits, he will renounce a society which sanctions such injustice and leave Paris to live the life of a hermit.

When the young courtier, Oronte, begs his opinion on some verses of which Oronte is the author, Alceste's rude and needless criticism adds another to the not inconsiderable list of his enemies and brings upon him the threat of a second lawsuit.

Now Alceste has the misfortune to love Célimène, a comely and popular young woman with little regard for the truth. Her main interest is to surround herself with admirers, each of whom she endeavors to persuade that he is the favored one. While Alceste is attempting to persuade Célimène openly to acknowledge their engagement, a pretended friend of Célimène's, Arsinoé by name, under pretense of the frankness that Alceste admires, exposes Célimène's falseness. Her other admirers drop away like flies. Not so Alceste. His lawsuit has finally been lost, and now he asks Célimène to prove her love by sharing the hermit's existence to which he plans to retire.

Célimène is willing to take Alceste's name in marriage to make up for the injury which she admits she has done the unquestioned sincerity of his regard. She confesses, however, that she is unwilling to leave Paris for she has no mind to forego the pleasures of youth and beauty for anyone's sake. This confession does for Alceste what Arsinoé's exposure failed to accomplish. The scales drop from his eyes and he sees Célimène for the flirt that she is.

Éliante, Célimène's cousin, had herself been in love with Alceste but since he announces a total lack of interest in women thenceforward, she contents herself with the love of his friend, Philinte. The play closes with this couple's stated determination to change Alceste's outlook on life.

Pierre Corneille

.. { *Born, Rouen, France, 1606* } ..
  { *Died, probably in Paris, 1684* }

CORNEILLE'S first play, *Mélite*, was presented in Paris in 1629 and at once scored a popular success. Like the playwright's other early efforts it was full of the insipid love that was the mode of the moment. These first plays of Corneille's, however, insipid as they were, were far superior to any French plays that preceded them. It is to these very plays, in fact, that modern drama owes the happy invention of the soubrette. But when the epoch-making *Cid* appeared in 1636 it so far outshone anything that preceded it, that the earlier plays were practically disregarded.

The critics and Corneille's contemporary writers waged around this revolutionary piece of dramatic writing as passionate a battle as raged around Hugo's *Hernani* some two centuries later. The public, however, spoke with no uncertain voice, and from *The Cid* modern French drama dates. It is quite possible that much of the criticism of *The Cid* was due to an awkwardness inherent in the play itself. Corneille as a dramatist adhered rigidly to the classical tradition of the three unities. The plot of *The Cid* was drawn from a Spanish source, and the Spaniards knew nothing of the three unities. Naturally the resulting combination was not entirely happy.

Corneille followed *The Cid* with other plays in a similar style, among them *Horace*, *Cinna*, and *Polyeucte*, which share with *The Cid* the best of his dramatic powers. His comedy, *Le Menteur*, ranks as the best French comedy prior to Molière. It was not, however, until eighteen years after his first dramatic success that he was finally elected to the French Academy. This tardiness was due, perhaps, in some measure to Richelieu's hostility.

Corneille's father was a magistrate and lawyer who was ennobled in the year following his son's great success with *The Cid*. The young Corneille was educated by the Jesuits and later studied law. He actually continued work in minor legal positions long after he became famous . . . in fact, until he was forty-four. For a time he enjoyed wealth and popularity, but the rising stars of Molière and Racine eclipsed his. They perfected the style in which Corneille had pioneered. A fickle public, ever ready to applaud newer celebrities, forgot or disregarded Corneille and he gradually was reduced to wretched circumstances. In 1663 he was granted a pension but its payment was irregular and he died in poverty.

In temperament Corneille was serious, rugged and stern; in manner he was awkward and ill at ease; but in the field of drama he was more than a successful writer; he was a pioneer, a trail blazer for the subsequent genius of Molière.

THE CID

First produced in Paris, probably late in November, 1636.

SCENE: *Seville.*

THE famous soldier, Diègue, had served King Fernand of Castile faithfully and well. In his old age he was rewarded with the coveted position of tutor to the young Prince. Since Gomez, Count of Gormaz, although considerably younger, had been scarcely less conspicuous for personal bravery and crafty generalship, he had believed that he would be chosen for this mark of honor. In his bitter disappointment he not only refused to sanction the marriage of Diègue's son, Roderick, to his daughter, Chimène, but offered deadly insult to Diègue by a blow in the face.

Since Diègue was too infirm to wield a sword in defense of his honor, it fell to Roderick's lot to avenge his father in a duel from which he emerged victorious. Knowing that by killing Chimène's father, he had sacrificed all hope of winning her, Roderick begged the girl to kill him. Although filial love and duty had impelled her to demand vengeance from the King, she could not kill the man she loved for obeying the dictates of honor. Meanwhile, since Roderick had made himself subject to arrest by a duel which the King had forbidden, Diègue persuaded his son secretly to head a band of trusty followers and to ambush the Moors who even at the moment were about to attempt a surprise attack. So well did Roderick acquit himself that even the two Sultans, captives of his prowess, acclaimed him Cid, the highest honor they could conceive. After this additional proof of loyalty and bravery, the King could do no less than forgive his young subject.

Chimène, however, still insisted on revenge. At length the King permitted her to name her other suitor, Sancho, to avenge her father in single combat with Roderick, naming her hand as the winner's reward.

Roderick's assurance that he would offer no resistance to death at the hands of her chosen champion, finally forced from Chimène the reluctant admission that only a sense of filial duty had impelled her to insist on vengeance. She begged him to rescue her from a hateful marriage.

When the duel was over and Sancho appeared, sword in hand, Chimène jumped to the conclusion that Roderick was dead. Falling on her knees before the King, she begged that she be released from the promise of marriage to enter a convent, bestowing her fortune on Sancho in reparation. As it turned out, Sancho had merely come to report that he was alive because Roderick had generously refused to take the life of one who loved Chimène. Thus both honor and love were satisfied.

Jean Racine

{Born, La Ferté Milon, France, 1639}
Died, Paris, 1699

THE reign of Louis XIV in France, like the Golden Age of Pericles in Athens, was remarkable for literary and dramatic work as well as for military achievements. In the field of drama, the three great names of the period . . . Corneille, Molière, and Racine . . . may be likened to the three Grecian dramatists: Æschylus, Sophocles and Euripides. Of the three it is probable that Racine most resembles Euripides in his happy facility of expression that commands audience for his dramas even when the ideas are commonplace.

Racine was the son of a minor government official and well connected. In the process of securing an education, the period between his sixteenth and his nineteenth years was spent in one of the rural branches of the famous Abbey of Port Royal. Young Jean did not take too kindly at the time to the religious environment. To prevent his spending so much time reading the "heathen" Greek dramatists and attempting to write poetry of his own, the fathers gave him the task of translating the Latin hymns of the Breviary into French verse. These three years, however, had a definite effect on the dramatic writings of his later life. In fact, they are probably directly responsible for the plays, *Esther* and *Athalie*, which were written after his retirement from public production.

The immediate and overwhelming success of his *Andromaque* on the stage of the Hôtel de Burgogne in Paris established him as a formidable rival for Corneille who at that time held the most prominent position in French dramatic circles. *Andromaque* is certainly one of Racine's best plays, and by some critics is regarded as his masterpiece. It is possible, however, that his later classical tragedy, *Phèdre*, should in reality be considered his most perfect piece of dramatic writing.

Phèdre was a comparative failure on the contemporary stage for two reasons: (1) the theme rather scandalized French audiences; (2) a clique headed by the powerful Duchesse of Boulogne into whose bad graces Racine had fallen set on foot a plan to damn the play. They not only bought up all the best seats at the theater where *Phèdre* was playing, but at another theater they started a rival play, named *Phèdre*, and written by a bookseller's hack.

This incident marked Racine's virtual retirement from the stage. The two religious plays, *Athalie* and *Esther*, were written upon request for private performance. Like Euripides, Racine left but one comedy, *Les Plaideurs* (*The Lawyers*). It is interesting to note that his first play, *Thebaïde*, was accepted and produced by Molière in 1664, when its author was but twenty-five.

ANDROMAQUE
(Andromache)

Produced at the Theater of the Hôtel de Burgogne in Paris in 1667.

SCENE: *A hall at the Palace of Pyrrhus in Buthrotum, a town of Epirus.*

WHEN the ten-year-long Trojan war ended, Andromaque, wife of the slain Hector, was given by lot to Pyrrhus, the son of Hector's slayer, Achilles. By means of a trick, Andromaque was able to save her infant son, Astyanax, also, and at the opening of the play Pyrrhus, who has fallen in love with his captive, has thus far permitted her to keep her son, hoping to forward his own suit with the mother.

The other Greek cities, alarmed by Pyrrhus's failure to kill Astyanax, have sent Orestes, Agamemnon's son, as ambassador to demand the death or surrender of the Trojan heir. Orestes has accepted the mission largely because it will give him an opportunity to see his cousin, Hermione, daughter of Helen and Menelaus, and affianced bride of Pyrrhus.

Although some time has passed since Hermione came to Epirus, no step has been taken toward the wedding ceremonies. Pyrrhus's infatuation with Andromaque has apparently caused him utterly to disregard his agreement with Menelaus. Hermione, who is as much in love with Pyrrhus as he with the Trojan princess, still lingers hoping for better fortune. Orestes, knowing the situation, hopes that in her disappointment Hermione will turn to him.

Since Andromaque continues to scorn Pyrrhus's suit, he finally tells her that unless she marries him he will kill Astyanax. Believing it the only way to save her son, Andromaque consents, intending to kill herself as soon as the ceremony is over, secure in the knowledge that Pyrrhus will keep his vow to be a father to her son.

At this final insult, Hermione experiences a mad desire for vengeance. She promises Orestes that if he will kill Pyrrhus at the marriage altar she will become his bride. Orestes feels that individual murder is quite a different matter from a vengeance wrought by united Greek armies. The thought of losing Hermione, however, is unbearable, and he bids his men kill Pyrrhus at the close of the marriage ceremony. When Orestes takes the news to Hermione, she meets him with a torrent of angry reproaches and rushes off to kill herself on her lover's dead body. This final shock, climaxing long continued strain, unbalances Orestes' mind . . . fortunately for his safety, for it gives his followers an opportunity to get him on board his ship before the anger of Pyrrhus's subjects can destroy them all.

ANDROMAQUE   ASTYANAX   HECUBE   PRIAN   HELENUS

Elizabethan "Plaie" House

Thomas Heywood

{ *Born, Lincolnshire, England, 1570–75* }
{ *Buried, Clerkenwell, England, 1641* }

THOMAS HEYWOOD in his preface to *The English Traveller* (1633) describes himself as having had "an entire hand or at least a main finger in 220 plays." Probably before the close of his career in 1641 this number was considerably increased. Only some twenty-four of these plays survive however, and surprisingly little definite information concerning the play-

wright's life is available. The first mention of him in a stage connection was by the theatrical manager, Philip Henslowe, who reported him as having written a play for the Lord Admiral's Company in October, 1596. In 1598 he appears to have been regularly engaged as an actor in the same company. Since no wages are mentioned and since it was customary in those days for troupes of actors to own their company cooperatively and share in the profits, if any, it is probable that this was the basis of his employment.

In addition to his regular plays, Thomas Heywood wrote many pageants and poems, and made translations from Sallust, Lucian and others. This last activity encourages the belief that he had at least some university education, probably at Cambridge. The best of his plays is a domestic drama entitled *A Woman Killed with Kindness*. This play which brings us close to the heart of English middle-class life, was one of the earlier dramas of domestic tragedy. Heywood's *The Wise Woman of Hogsdon* portrays English low life almost as successfully as the former play dealt with the middle class. He is credited, also, with three admirable comedies of adventure . . . *The Captives*, *The Fair Maid of the West*, and *Fortune by Land and Sea*.

Charles Lamb has called Heywood a "prose Shakspere."[1] He delighted in a broad, coarse farce. He had a keen eye for dramatic situations. His constructive skill, however, was meager when it came to smooth amalgamation of the by-plots he insisted on introducing into many of his plays. While these by-plots were frequently good in themselves, they invariably detracted from the unity and effectiveness of the play as a whole. His power of characterization, too, was weak. The background and settings for his plays, however, are as a rule excellently chosen and realistically portrayed. All in all Heywood was a versatile writer, holding his own in romantic drama, chronicle history and the comedy of manners. Thomas Heywood is important today, therefore, not so much for the plays themselves that have come down to us, as that he is another link in that process of achieving complete freedom from the shackles of classical convention on the English stage.

[1] In his *Dramatic Essays*.

A WOMAN KILLED WITH KINDNESS

Probably performed in London in 1603.

SCENE: *Rural England.*

MISTRESS ANNE FRANKFORD is a paragon of grace, beauty, and all wifely virtues, while her husband, Master John, is kindness itself and deeply in love with his new wife. All this augurs well for a long and happy married life. But Master Frankford foolishly takes into his household Master Wendoll, an impoverished gentleman to whom he has taken a liking. Master Wendoll is unable to resist the charms of his friend's wife and persuades her to accept him as a lover.

Meanwhile, Mistress Frankford's brother, Sir Francis Acton, quarrels with Sir Charles Mountford over a wager. In the heat of anger, Sir Charles kills two of Sir Francis's men and is thrown into prison. It takes his entire patrimony, excepting only the family estate to pay damages and win release. Even then the murder charge still hangs over him.

One, Cramwell, pretending friendship, offers Sir Charles a sum of money to rehabilitate his fortunes. This gift turns out to be merely a ruse to force Sir Charles to sell the estate. When he refuses, yet cannot return Cramwell's money, he is again put in irons.

Meanwhile, Sir Francis has fallen in love with Sir Charles' sister, Susan. She, however, scorns both his addresses and his proffers of help. Although he cannot forward his suit with the lady, Sir Francis magnanimously pays all Sir Charles' debts and drops the charge of murder. When investigation shows Sir Charles to whom he owes his release, he persuades his sister to pay his obligations by offering Sir Francis her honor, never dreaming Sir Francis would accept a dowerless bride. When Sir Francis refuses to take Susan except as his wife, she is feign to relent and love him for his generous spirit. Thus the two families are reconciled.

Meanwhile, of course, Master Frankford discovers his wife's infidelity and banishes her from his sight to one of his manors several miles away. Here she has all the material comforts but starves herself to death in remorse. Just before she dies, her brother and his bride, with other mutual friends, persuade Master Frankford to see his wife once more. Convinced of the sincerity of her repentance, he acknowledges her again as his wife, and all agree that it was his extreme kindness that showed her the enormity of her offense and made her resolve to kill herself. As a final token of esteem her husband promises a tribute of his forgiveness on her gravestone.

The Old Globe Theatre, London

Ben Jonson

Born, probably Westminster, 1574
Died, probably London, 1637

BEN JONSON, like Beaumont and Fletcher, and a host of other English writers, was a part of that famous Mermaid Tavern group of which Shakspere was, even in those days, easily the outstanding figure. But if Shakspere was first, Ben Jonson was certainly second both in the quality of his genius and the amount of work he turned out.

Jonson had been a soldier in Flanders, and an actor and hack writer for Philip Henslowe, the first famous English theatrical manager. To this he shortly added the glory of an appointment as poet-laureate. But it is as a dramatist that posterity is most interested in Jonson. His plays fall roughly into three classes: realistic comedies, tragedies and masques. As a contribution both to the contemporary stage and to the evolution of drama, the realistic comedies are the most important. The play, *Every Man in His Humour*, produced in 1598, inaugurated a new style of comedy unlike anything that had been seen on the English stage. It dealt, not with the passions of mankind, but with their little everyday follies and foibles. It was the sensation of the day and was enacted before the queen by the company of players to which Shakspere belonged.

Jonson's skill probably reached its apex in the anti-Puritanical satire, *Bartholomew Fair*. This play is a critical analysis of current manners and is not only masterly but essentially original.

Learned and brilliant as he was, Jonson appears to have been neither genial nor lovable. The analytical mind that could so clearly limn the weaknesses of his contemporaries, was utterly lacking in sympathy for those weaknesses or for the people in whom they appeared. As a dramatist, Jonson was resourceful in the creation of character; as a practical man of the theater, he was clever in the invention of comic situations. His keen wit and robust humor founded in his day an entirely new dramatic movement. But they did more. They wielded an influence on the works of succeeding writers for the English-speaking stage, that is felt right up to the present time.

An imposing list of Jonson's plays are still read by students of English drama. The better known, in addition to the two mentioned above, are: *Every Man Out of His Humour*, *Cynthia's Revels* (written during the War of the Theaters), *The Poetaster* (also part of the ammunition of the same literary squabble), *The Case Is Altered*, *A Tale of a Tub*, *The Alchemist*, *Epicœne*, *The Devil's an Ass*, *The New Inn*, *The Magnetic Lady*, and *The Staple of News*.

BARTHOLOMEW FAIR

Produced in London in 1614.

SCENE: *The home of the Littlewits; the grounds of Bartholomew Fair.*

ALTHOUGH the annual Bartholomew Fair is considered an improper place for gentle-folk to go, young Mrs. Littlewit and her husband, John, concoct a scheme whereby they get permission of Mrs. Littlewit's mother, Dame Purecraft, and the approval of the latter's current suitor, Zeal-of-the-land Busy. Grace Wellborn, Justice Overdo's ward, and her fiancé, the foolish Bartholomew Cokes, do not feel the need of an excuse, taking the attitude that aristocrats can go anywhere. So off to the Fair they go, chaperoned by Dame Overdo. Also among the visitors to the Fair are Gentleman Winwife and his companion, Tom Quarlous, the gamester.

In former years Justice Adam Overdo has depended on spies to report improper doings. This year, however, he has made up his mind that he will visit the Fair in disguise and obtain his evidence firsthand. No one, he believes, can put anything over on a man so keen as himself. He promptly takes a fancy to a smooth-spoken youth, named Edgworth, and never realizes that he is a pickpocket operating under the Justice's very nose, even when the Justice himself lands in the stocks accused of the crime.

Meanwhile, Grace, separated from her party, falls in with Winwife and Quarlous. So anxious is she to be rid of the foolish Cokes that she promises to marry whichever of the two men can write the prettiest word on her tablet. The first passer-by is to mark his choice and Grace agrees to make it known when the Fair is over. The selection is duly made by the harmless madman, Trouble-all, but Quarlous is unwilling to wait until evening to know his fate. Stealing Trouble-all's ragged costume he reappears and contrives to learn that the successful word is Winwife's.

Now it happens that a few days previous a fortune teller had bidden the credulous Dame Purecraft to marry a madman. When she spies Quarlous in Trouble-all's clothes she beseeches him to marry her and the gamester, having lost Grace, is not averse to annexing Dame Purecraft's wealth.

Toward the end of the day all the characters drift into a puppet show and there Justice Overdo reveals his identity. When he learns how thoroughly he has been taken in by Edgworth and that the masked bawd he is about to sentence is his own wife, he reflects that he is as subject to human weakness as the rest of mankind, and the subsequent dinner is "on him."

The Fortune Theatre, London

Beaumont and Fletcher

}.. *Francis Beaumont, Born, 1584.   Died, 1616* }..
John Fletcher, Born, 1579.   Died, 1625

ALTHOUGH collaboration between writers was common in Shaksperian England, the success of the literary partnership between Francis Beaumont and John Fletcher was so unique that their names have been indissolubly connected. Both of them were of upper class birth and both belonged to the group of writers and playwrights that frequented the Mermaid Tavern. It was the same group to which Shakspere and Ben Jonson belonged. In fact, Shakspere is known to have collaborated with Fletcher in at least one play, *The Two Noble Kinsmen.*

Beaumont was born in Grace-Dieu, Leicestershire, where his father was a justice of the commons pleas. His formal education at what is now known as Pembroke College, and later at Oxford, for some reason did not result in a degree. At the age of twenty young Beaumont was admitted to the Inner Temple, one of the four ancient guilds of the legal profession. Acceptance in one of these guilds was equivalent to modern admission to the bar. There is no record, however, that Beaumont ever had a client or tried a case.

It was probably about 1606 that he became acquainted with Fletcher. Almost at once they recognized each other as kindred spirits and from that time until Beaumont's marriage in 1613 they lived in the same house.

Fletcher's father was a clergyman, incumbent in Rye, Sussex, at the time of John's birth, but afterwards made Bishop of London. The records of Fletcher's youth and education are even more meager than those of Beaumont's. He apparently attended Corpus Christi College, Cambridge, but for how long we do not know. Nor do we know whether or not he ever received a degree. For both these men prominence came only after the beginning of their friendship and collaboration.

Altogether the two men wrote about fifty-four plays. On the whole their work is clever and gay, rarely sounding the depths of passion or serious feeling. Their characterizations are merely surface descriptions. The stage of their day was vulgar in the extreme, and these two writers saw no reason to become exceptions. The language and situations in most of their plays is far from pure. Indeed, it would scarcely be tolerated even on the uncensored stage of today. The songs scattered throughout their plays, on the other hand, almost rival Shakspere for sweetness and beauty.

The best results of this famous collaboration are represented by *Philaster, The Maid's Tragedy, The Faithful Shepherdess, The Knight of the Burning Pestle,* and *A King and No King.* In the first two Beaumont's genius is dominant while *The Faithful Shepherdess* is a beautiful pastoral drama written mostly by Fletcher.

PHILASTER or LOVE LIES BLEEDING

Probably produced in London about 1608.

SCENE: *Sicily.*

THE King of Calabria slew the ruler of Sicily and seized his throne. He would have imprisoned the popular Prince Philaster except that he feared an uprising. He made plans, however, to secure the succession of his house to the Sicilian throne by marrying his only child, Arethusa, to the powerful Prince Pharamond of Spain.

Knowing that the dethroned Philaster would not avow his love for her, Arethusa confessed her love to him. Overjoyed, Philaster gave her his page boy, Bellario, to act as messenger between them while Arethusa should contrive release from her distasteful engagement. She found opportunity when her lady-in-waiting overheard Pharamond make a rendezvous with the wanton Megra. When the King surprised the couple, Megra in retaliation accused Arethusa of improper relations with Bellario. With intent to turn Philaster to more warlike thoughts, Lord Dion supported the charge claiming to have been an eyewitness.

The disillusioned Philaster promptly lost interest in both love and war. He refused to take back the page, Bellario, whom the King had forced Arethusa to dismiss and thought only of self-destruction. In her despair, Arethusa's thoughts were turned toward the same end. Contriving to lose herself from the royal hunt on the following day, she was about to take her life when Philaster discovered her. Because the young prince believed her faithless he was ready to accede to her request that he kill her, intending then to kill himself. The interference of a country yokel, however, put Philaster to flight. He was traced by the blood from his wounds and Bellario, seeing him in danger, undertook to save him by falsely confessing that he had attacked Arethusa out of a desire for revenge.

Through this generous action Philaster was convinced of the innocence of both Arethusa and Bellario. To the complete dismay of Arethusa, he came out of hiding and surrendered. Under pretense of a desire for vengeance, the Princess persuaded the King to remand both prisoners in her charge. So it happened that when the King was about to behead Philaster, he discovered that the Prince had become his son-in-law. His Majesty promptly imprisoned the young couple, but was forced almost at once to release Philaster that he might put down a popular uprising in his behalf, and rescue Pharamond from death at the hands of the mob.

For his success in this undertaking the King rewarded Philaster with the return of his kingdom and blessings on his marriage. At the same time, Bellario was revealed as Lord Dion's daughter, turned page boy for love of Philaster. The generous Arethusa promptly made her a lady-in-waiting that as a reward for loyalty she might always be near her King.

Arethusa

Joseph Addison

.·{ *Born, 1672, Milford, Wiltshire, England* }·.
   Died, 1719, Kensington, England

JOSEPH ADDISON is remembered today for the charming sketches of that delightful, imaginary figure, *Roger de Coverley*, rather than for his single drama, *Cato*. Indeed, the immediate success and continuing popularity of the play with 18th century audiences is hard to understand, considering its total lack of dramatic power. It was, of course, beautifully phrased and filled with lofty and tender sentiment, characteristics which had a wide fashionable appeal for contemporary society. So skillfully did Addison express himself that both

political parties acclaimed the play and attempted to read into it some political significance. Its reception was enthusiastic and it was promptly translated into several foreign languages.

Addison, the successful journalist, poet and playwright of 1713 (the year of Cato's production) had put a world between himself and the boy, Addison, of his college days. The Addison of Queen's College, Oxford, and later of Magdalen College, was unbelievably shy but distinguished even at this early age for the degree of his scholarship. Perhaps it was partially this shyness as well as his poverty and the religious tendencies inherited from his clergyman father that brought him to the point of taking religious orders after his graduation.

His facility in writing original Latin verse, however, had attracted notice in influential quarters and at a timely moment he was granted a royal pension of sufficient size to enable him to travel on the continent. Shortly after his return came the memorable victory of Blenheim. The English ministry wished to commemorate the triumph in verse and commissioned Addison to the task. Before the resultant poem, *The Campaign*, was completely finished, it had secured such approval that he was appointed Commissioner of Appeals and shortly afterwards Under-Secretary of State.

With his living secured, he was free to turn his attention to literature. One of his early ventures was *The Tatler*, a periodical which he published in company with Sir Richard Steele. Shortly after this journal suspended publication it was succeeded by the better known *Spectator*, another periodical, in which the famous *Roger de Coverley* made his appearance. At the same time, Addison wrote numerous political pieces, essays and poems, as well as his tragedy, *Cato*. Apparently he found time from his writing for the little courtesies of courtship, for in 1716, three years before his death he married Charlotte, Dowager Countess of Warwick. The marriage, however, is reputed to have been an unhappy one.

Posterity credits Joseph Addison with doing more than any other man of his time toward creating a wide public for literature.

CATO

Produced in London, April 13, 1713, and ran for 35 nights.

SCENE: *Utica, where Cato the Younger, as leader of those still faithful to Republican Rome is making his last stand against the victorious Caesar.*

THE Roman Senator, Sempronius, is convinced that further resistance to Caesar is futile. In the Senate, however, he is loud in his praises of Cato's determination to resist to the end. Meanwhile, behind Cato's back, he is attempting to stir up mutiny. He has persuaded certain of the Roman soldiers to his way of thinking. He has also induced Syphax, general of the Numidian mercenaries, to plan a bolt to Caesar's camp together with all his troops.

Juba, Prince of the Numidians, however, reveres Cato as a father and teacher. He is, moreover, in love with Cato's daughter, Marcia, so that all attempts by Syphax to dissuade him from supporting Cato fail. To complicate the issues of love and battle still further, Cato's sons, Marcus and Portius are both in love with Lucia, daughter of the loyal Senator Lucius. She cannot bear to wound Marcus by accepting Portius, so resolves to wed neither one.

When Caesar is encamped not far from Utica, he sends messengers to offer amnesty and high honor to Cato if he will but lay down his arms and become a follower of Caesar. Cato proudly refuses, preferring death to submission. Sempronius has by now completed his plans for going over to Caesar. His suit for Marcia's hand has met with no encouragement, so now he resolves, before he goes, to ravish her. With the help of Syphax he disguises himself as Juba and, surrounding himself with Juba's faithless bodyguard, gains entrance to Marcia's apartments. His plan would have succeeded but for Juba's timely appearance, almost immediately following the entrance of Sempronius. In a brief fight, Juba kills the impostor and then betakes himself to Cato to describe what has happened.

When Marcia enters the hall and sees what she supposes is Juba's dead body, she is overcome with grief. She is proclaiming her love for the dead prince when the live Juba returns and overhears her. The young couple's happiness is interrupted by the arrival of Portius with the news that Syphax, on hearing of Sempronius' death, had charged the gate with his Numidian troops in an attempt to escape to Caesar's camp. Marcus, in defending the gate, had received his death wounds, but not before he had dispatched the traitor, Syphax. The death of Marcus leaves Portius and Lucia free to acknowledge their love.

Cato, however, worn out with the disasters to his beloved Rome, and heartbroken by the treason of false friends, ends his life just as news comes that slaughtered Pompey's son is arriving to aid him with fresh troops.

Oliver Goldsmith

..{ *Born, Elphin, Roscommon, Ireland, 1728* }..
  Died, London, England, 1774

AFTER a course at Trinity College, Dublin,
made miserable by his personal ungainli-
ness and bad manners, Oliver Goldsmith was on
the point of emigrating to America. If he had
not missed his ship, high school students might
not find in their course of prescribed reading
such literary gems as *The Deserted Village* and
The Vicar of Wakefield, nor play lovers enjoy the
absurdities of his dramatic masterpiece, *She
Stoops to Conquer*.

But if the keynote of Goldsmith's character
was improvidence, there seems, during his
youth at any rate, always to have been a helping
hand to rescue him from the penalties of that
improvidence. After he missed the boat to
America, he was given 50 pounds with which to
devote himself to the study of law. His intentions were doubtless good, but the money he
lost in gambling. Subsequently he was again
"endowed," this time that he might study
medicine. For a year and a half he made a half-
hearted pretense of interest. Then Wanderlust
seized him and he became a continental tramp
earning a bare subsistence by means of his flute.

Coming to London in 1756 he became a
literary hack, writing brilliantly, albeit super-
ficially, on any subject that offered promise of
keeping him out of a debtor's cell. Carelessness,
intemperance and gambling brought him into
debt at a time when he should have been most
prosperous. Thus it was that from a background of worry and ill health his famous
comedy was written, inspired, it is said, by an
incident of his own youth.

Just at the close of a school term he had been
given a small sum of money. He determined to
celebrate with a new experience, that of spending the night at an inn in the course of his home-
ward journey. He stopped off in a small town
through which the stage passed, and by chance
it was the local wit whom he asked for direction to an inn. This wag directed him to the
house of a prosperous squire. The family fell in
with the joke and young Goldsmith with considerable swagger actually did spend the night
in the house.

For a time it seemed doubtful whether this
comedy would ever reach production, so absolutely contrary was it to all accepted tenets of
the contemporary stage. When it was finally
accepted and staged, however, it enjoyed an
immediate and lasting success. In fact, this play
sounded the keynote of Goldsmith's "mission"
. . . to render more natural the comedy of his
time and to strike a decisive blow at the "gen-
teel" or "sentimental" comedy of his contemporaries.

SHE STOOPS TO CONQUER or THE MISTAKES OF A NIGHT

Produced March 15, 1773, at the Covent Garden Theater, London.

SCENE: *The old-fashioned house of the Hardcastles in the English countryside, with a brief interlude in the village inn.*

SQUIRE HARDCASTLE'S second wife is quite determined that her spoiled and not too brilliant son, Tony Lumpkin, shall marry her niece, Constance Neville. In this way she will be enabled to keep in the family Miss Neville's fortune which consists of a casket of valuable jewels. The young people, however, have other plans, especially Miss Neville who is secretly pledged to one, Hastings.

Mr. Hardcastle, likewise, has plans for his own charming daughter, Kate, whom he wishes to marry to the son of his old friend, Sir Charles Marlow. It is young Marlow's misfortune to be dumb in the presence of ladies of his own social status. He is, however, a master of clever repartee when talking to bar maids and girls of like station.

The Hardcastle family are momentarily expecting the arrival of young Marlow and his friend, Hastings. The approaching travellers stop at the village inn to inquire their way. Tony Lumpkin, who is there as usual with his cronies, conceives the idea of persuading the young men that they have lost their way and will have to spend the night at an inn. He directs them to the Hardcastle house which he highly recommends if they will excuse the eccentricities of the owner and his family.

Neither young Marlow nor Squire Hardcastle senses that both are victims of a hoax and the squire is much incensed at the bold and impudent behavior of his friend's son. Young Hastings, as soon as he sees Constance, puts two and two together. This pair agree to keep Marlow in ignorance and pretend that Constance and Kate simply happen to be stopping the night at the inn.

When introduced to Kate young Marlow can find little to say and stumbles over that. In his embarrassment he never once looks at her face. It is not surprising, therefore, that later in the evening when he sees her going about the house in the plain house dress her father insists on, he takes her for the bar maid. She encourages the deception in order to find out if he is really as witless as he seems. In her bar maid's guise she is pleasantly surprised to find him not dumb but, indeed, possessed of a graceful and ready wit. When she reveals herself as a well born but poor relation of the Hardcastle family he acknowledges his love for her.

Further comic situations are created by Tony's attempts to help Constance and her lover elope with her casket of jewels. When through ludicrous misunderstandings these come to naught, Squire Hardcastle benignly sets everything right for both pairs of lovers.

Richard Brinsley Butler Sheridan

..{ *Born, Dublin, Ireland, 1751*
Died, London, England, 1816 }..

RICHARD BRINSLEY SHERIDAN seems to
have had two good plays, one good opera,
and one good oration in his system. His life,
aside from that, boils down to twenty years of
fashionable life in London as a dabbler in
politics, the companion of dissolute princes and
a wastrel. At the age of 21, following a romantic elopement, he married and set up housekeeping in London on a grand scale with no
money and no prospects except his wife's dowry.
The young couple, nevertheless, entered the
fashionable world and apparently held up their
end in entertaining.

Sheridan's lucky star was in the ascendant,
however, for on January 17, 1775, at the Covent
Garden Theater, *The Rivals* was produced. The
first performance was not a success. It was too
long and the part of Sir Lucius O'Trigger was
poorly played. On January 28, a second performance proved a complete success, establishing
both play and playwright in the favor of
fashionable London.

The following year Sheridan, his father-in-
law (the composer, Thomas Finley) and Dr.
Ford bought a half interest in the Drury Lane
theater and in 1778 became sole owners.
Shortly after the success of *The Rivals* Sheridan
with the help of his father-in-law produced the
opera, *The Duenna*. This piece was accorded
such a warm reception that it played for seventy-
five performances.

On May 8, 1777, Sheridan directed his masterpiece, *A School for Scandal*, in the Drury Lane
theater of which he was now manager, with Mrs.
Abington in the rôle of *Lady Teazle*. The play
lacks the unity that marks *The Rivals*, and it
does not have the same wealth of broadly
humorous incident. Of the many "screen"
scenes of dramatic history, however, the one in
School for Scandal is by far the cleverest, while the
"auction" scene is a success on any stage.

In 1880 Sheridan entered Parliament as the
ally of Charles James Fox on the side of the
American Colonials. He is said to have paid the
burgesses of Stafford five guineas apiece for the
honor of representing them. As a consequence,
his first speech in Parliament had to be a defense
against the charge of bribery.

During the bitter political controversies of the
period Sheridan was practically the only man in
Parliament who was never challenged to a duel
. . . this, in spite of the sharp and effective
weapon of ridicule he constantly wielded. When
finally he failed of reelection to Parliament his
creditors closed in on him and his last years were
harassed by debt and disappointment. In the
course of events the American Congress offered
Sheridan 20,000 pounds in recognition of his
efforts to prevent the Revolutionary War. To
his eternal credit is recorded the refusal of this
gift.

A SCHOOL FOR SCANDAL

Produced at the Drury Lane Theater, London, May 8, 1777

SCENE: *Contemporary London.*

THE middle-aged and wealthy bachelor, Sir Peter Teazle, has married the young and comely daughter of a country squire. The fashionable society of which Lady Teazle through her marriage becomes a part, occupies itself mainly with malicious gossip whose arrows no one, however chaste, can completely escape. By far the most dangerous of these backbiting cliques is the one led by Lady Sneerwell.

This lady is attempting through lies and letters written by the forger, Snake, to break up the love affair between Charles Surface and Sir Peter's ward, Maria, hoping to get Charles for herself. To this end she has joined forces with Charles's brother, Joseph, a hypocritical youth who enjoys an excellent reputation in contrast to his brother's wild and extravagant habits. Joseph has his eye on the fortune that will one day come to Maria and is backed in his suit by Sir Peter who has been utterly fooled by the young man's righteous exterior. Maria sees through Joseph, however, and turns a cold ear in spite of her guardian's expressed wishes.

Meanwhile Sir Oliver Surface arrives unexpectedly from Australia. He hears such conflicting reports of his nephews and prospective heirs that he decides to look them over before he makes his arrival known. He approaches Charles in the guise of money lender and in the famous "auction" scene buys the family portraits. Throughout the transaction he is impressed with Charles's high sense of honor and obligation to those less fortunate. When he approaches Joseph as a poor relation begging help, Joseph is revealed in his true colors.

Now gossip has linked Lady Teazle's name with that of Charles Surface, but in reality she has been indulging for fashion's sake in an affair with Joseph. The rumors about Lady Teazle and Charles come at last to Sir Peter's ears and, much distressed, he goes to Joseph's apartment to consult with him. Lady Teazle, who is enjoying a tryst with Joseph, sees Sir Peter's arrival and hastily hides behind a screen. Sir Peter, in turn, hides in a closet, when Charles unexpectedly arrives. The latter inadvertently reveals Lady Teazle behind the screen and Sir Peter, coming out of his closet, revises his estimate of Joseph.

Lady Teazle throws herself on Sir Peter's mercy with the frank confession that she was pretending to an affair because it was the fashion, but admits that her only real interest is in her own husband. Sir Oliver, meanwhile, has rounded up Snake, the forger. His confession brings about a reconciliation between Charles and Maria, and Sir Peter gladly withdraws his objections to this match.

François Marie Arouet

(Voltaire)

..{ *Born, Paris, France, 1694*
Died, Paris, 1778 }..

THIS brilliant playwright is known to the world today not by his own name, but simply as "Voltaire," the name he adopted after the successful production of his first play, *Œdipe*, in 1718. He was the son of a middle class family and was educated by Jesuit priests. From his earliest youth he seems to have been imbued with a spirit of scepticism and rebellion against intolerance. This characteristic which he was at no pains to hide, twice brought him im-prisonment in the Bastille, and at a later date, periods of exile from France.

One such exile in England brought Voltaire the acquaintance of the important contemporary English writers. Indeed, his writings were bringing him such fame outside of France that he corresponded with some of the greatest people of the day including Catherine the Great of Russia. About this time he spent several years in Berlin whither he had gone at the invitation of Frederick the Great of Prussia. During his stay in Berlin, Lessing, who was later to become the first great German dramatist, was employed by Voltaire in making translations.

The play, *Œdipe*, was written when Voltaire was but nineteen. Its production five years later gave him almost at once first place among living French dramatists. Voltaire had the supreme dramatic gift of portraying sharp conflict and this is the secret of the success of his best tragedies: "the conflict between patriot-ism and love in *Brutus;* between love and religious duty in *Zaïre;* between love and filial obedience in *Alzire* and *Tancrede.*"[1] If a love interest was not present in the plot Voltaire purposed to borrow, he nearly always invented one or borrowed one from some other source. He was the first playwright, too, to draw plot material from such distant and little known sources as China and South America.

At various times during his literary career Voltaire produced about a dozen comedies. From a very slight study of these it is obvious that his forte lay in tragedy rather than in the lighter touch required by comedy.

In his younger days Voltaire expressed a great admiration for Shakspere, but as his own posi-tion as a dramatist and critic became more firmly established, he seemed to think that to belittle Shakspere made Voltaire greater. Actually Vol-taire lacked the understanding and sympathy which are essential to the great dramatist; but he could give theatrical credence to a thrilling story and at the same time preach a sermon. As a dramatist, Voltaire was not great; as the standard bearer of intellectual freedom, his in-fluence is immeasurable.

Of the dramas which he produced, the two tragedies, *Zaïre* and *Mérope* are rated the best.

[1]Martha Bellinger in *A Short History of the Drama.*

ZAÏRE (*Zara*)

First production, August 13, 1732.

SCENE: *Jerusalem in the age of the Crusades.*

ZARA and Nerestan, Christian slaves, had grown up in the palace of Osman, Sultan of Turkey. Zara was but a baby when she was brought to the palace. In fact, the only proof that she was a Christian lay in the ornamental cross she wore. Consequently she had found no difficulty in accepting the Moslem faith. Nerestan, however, though but a young lad when captured, took his obligations to Christianity and his fellow slaves seriously. Two years before the opening of the play he had secured from the Sultan permission to go to France to seek ransom for his comrades, promising on his honor to return.

After his departure, Zara, budding into a lovely womanhood, fell deeply in love with the splendid young Osman. When she discovered that her love was requited and that Osman would make her his only wife and empress, her happiness was complete. On the day of her appointed nuptials, Nerestan returned from his long absence. He had been able to secure ransom for ten Christians only, but was willing to become again a slave if Zara were included in the ten. Even the hundred slaves freed through the Sultan's generosity, Nerestan included, did not make up for his bitter disillusionment when he found that Zara was about to marry the Sultan. He was gravely disappointed, too, that the Sultan had not felt it politic to release the aged Lusignan, descendant of the ancient kings of Jerusalem.

Zara, however, pleaded so successfully for the old man that presently she was enabled herself to conduct him, a free man, to join Nerestan's party. Through the cross she was wearing as an ornament, Lusignan recognized her as the baby daughter lost in the sack of Jerusalem by the Moslems. By means of certain scars, he likewise identified Nerestan as his son.

Horrified at the thought of Zara's proposed marriage to a Moslem, the two men obtained from her the promise that she would be baptized that day in Nerestan's presence and follow the priest's instructions. They also made her swear to keep the whole affair secret from Osman until they were gone.

Zara's plea that their nuptials be delayed for a day roused Osman's suspicions. The interception of Nerestan's letter bidding Zara meet him that night convinced the Sultan that she was faithless. Going himself to the appointed place, he stabbed the girl and had Nerestan seized. Only then did he learn the story and, unable to forgive his own lack of faith in his beloved, stabbed himself with the dagger that killed her.

Salvini as "Orosmane"

Gotthold Lessing

.·{ *Born, Kamenz, Germany, 1729* }··
.·{ *Died, Brunswick, Germany, 1781* }··

GOTTHOLD EPHRAIM LESSING, the first
of the truly German dramatists, was born
in a Lutheran clergyman's family. As was a
frequent custom in clergymen's families, his
father looked after his early education, later
sending him to a famous school at Meissen.
So apt a pupil was young Lessing that at 16 he
was ready for the University of Leipzig.

At the university he studied theology, then
medicine, and later on literature and philosophy.
But already he had made a connection with the
stage through translating French plays for
Frau Neuber's theater. In 1748 Frau Neuber

put on Lessing's own maiden effort, *Der Junge
Gelehrte*. From that time on, regardless of his
financial fortunes, Lessing gave his entire interest to some form of writing. For a time he
was employed in making translations by Voltaire, who was at this time living in Germany.
This contact, however, soon ended in disagree-
ment, according to some authorities, because
Lessing betrayed a literary confidence of Voltaire's.

The friendship could not have lasted long at
any rate, because Lessing soon found his own
dramatic beliefs directly opposed in principle to
Voltaire's pseudo-classicism. His revolt against
the Voltairean school is expressed in practical
fashion in his first important play, *Miss Sara
Sampson* (1755), a bourgeois tragedy of epoch-
making importance to the German stage.

In 1767 Lessing's famous *Minna von Barnhelm*
appeared, the first German comedy with characters and action concerned with contemporary
German life. Up to now, Lessing's income had
been so independable that he had not even considered marriage. In 1770, however, he was
made court librarian for the Duke of Brunswick
at Wolfenbuttel. With an income thus assured
he married, only to lose his wife and an infant
son within two years. To assuage his grief, he
plunged more deeply than ever into literary
work. He completed during this period the remarkable prose tragedy, *Emilia Galotti*, and
wrote the powerful *Nathan the Wise*, a play
which departed decidedly from precedent in its
choice of subject.

Lessing was not only the first truly German
playwright, but he is known, too, as the "father
of German criticism." Notable among his
critical works is the celebrated *Hamburg Drama-
turgy* which should have added materially to its
author's income. That it did not lay in the fact
that its excellence was immediately realized and
it was promptly pirated. The *Laökoön*, another
critical work, took for its subject the fields of
poetry and painting.

Lessing's literary activity continued with un-
impaired mental vigor right up to the time of
his sudden death while on a trip to Brunswick
in 1781.

MINNA VON BARNHELM

First produced in Hamburg, Germany, in 1767, but was not successful. When produced in Berlin the following year, it enjoyed immediate popularity.

SCENE: *An inn in the Prussian capital.*

MAJOR VON TELLHEIM is a discharged and disabled army officer. His penniless condition is due to the fact that repayment of a large sum advanced to the government during the recent war, is being held up and his honor in making the loan questioned. During Tellheim's absence from the inn the landlord has caused Tellheim's effects to be removed, ostensibly because his rooms were needed for a lady and her maid. In reality, the landlord doubts Tellheim's ability to pay, since he is already somewhat in arrears.

In the removal of the Major's possessions, the landlord comes upon a sealed envelope marked as containing five hundred thalers. This discovery makes him anxious to placate Tellheim. What he does not know is that the money has been left with the Major by Paul Werner, his former sergeant. Werner knowing Tellheim's predicament is in hope that he will use the money as his own. Tellheim is too honorable to borrow when he has no assurance of repaying. Instead, he bids his servant, Just, take his last possession of value, an expensive ring, and pawn it to satisfy the landlord's bill and his own back wages.

Just pledges the ring with the landlord but refuses to accept either wages or dismissal on the plea that he is in Tellheim's debt and will have to work it out. The garrulous landlord shows the ring to his newly arrived guests, revealing considerable concerning the owner's circumstances. The lady, Minna von Barnhelm, recognizes the ring as one of the betrothal rings which she and Tellheim had exchanged, and is overjoyed that her search for her missing lover is ended.

When Tellheim appears, however, he refuses to accept her hand or to continue the engagement on account of his precarious circumstances. When no argument can move him, Minna with the help of her maid, Franziska, pretends that she, too, is penniless and in dire straits. Under these circumstances Tellheim immediately claims the privilege of marrying and protecting her.

At this point a delayed letter from the King is delivered. It announces the restoration of Tellheim's fortune and the vindication of his honor. To punish him for making her suffer, Minna now pretends that she cannot marry Tellheim because of the inequality of their circumstances. In answer to his pleas, she uses his own recent arguments to confound him. Only when Tellheim is reduced to the verge of despair and the belated arrival of Minna's uncle and guardian threatens to give the whole thing away does Minna relent and reveal the truth. In a final scene of celebration matters are settled to the satisfaction of everyone including Franziska and Paul Werner who have discovered a lively interest in each other.

Minna von Barnhelm

Johann Wolfgang von Goethe

..{ *Born, Frankfort-on-Main, Germany, 1749* }..
{ *Died, Weimar, Germany, 1832* }

THE boy, Goethe, was a precocious young-ster. At the early age of eight he had already acquired some knowledge of Greek, Latin, French and Italian. He had likewise acquired from his mother the knack of story telling; and from a toy puppet show in his nursery his first interest in the stage.

Goethe's early education was somewhat irregular and informal, and already he was marked by that apparent feeling of superiority that stayed by him throughout his life. When he was about 16 he was sent to Leipzig, ostensibly to study law. He apparently studied more life than law and put in his time expressing his reactions through some form of writing. On at least two occasions, this form was dramatic.

Finally, in 1770 Goethe went to Strassburg, this time really intent on passing his preliminary examinations in law, and with the somewhat more frivolous ambition of learning to dance. Along with his study of law, he studied art, music, anatomy and chemistry. A strong friendship with the writer, Herder, was likewise no part of Goethe's experience at this time, a contact which was of considerable importance in these formative years.

In 1771 Goethe returned to Frankfort, nominally to practice law, but he was soon deep in work on what was to be his first dramatic success, *Götz von Berlichingen*. While this was actually the story of a robber baron of the 16th century it really represented Goethe's youthful protest against the established order and his demand for intellectual freedom. Its success made its hitherto unknown author the literary leader of Germany.

Goethe's invitation in 1775 to the court of Duke Karl August at Weimar was a turning point in the literary life of Germany. He became manager of the Court Theater, and interested himself in various other activities, so that for a period of some ten years not much actual writing was done.

The writing of *Faust*, however, that best known of Goethe's works, extended over practically the whole of Goethe's literary life, a period of 57 years. It was finally finished when Goethe was 81. *Faust* is in reality a dramatic poem rather than a piece for the stage. While based on the same legend as Marlowe's *Dr. Faustus*, it far transcends both its legendary source and the English play. The latter is little more than a Morality illustrating the punishment of sin; Goethe's work is a drama of redemption.

Others of Goethe's works which have stood the test of time include: *Clavigo, Egmont, Stella, Iphigenia in Tauris* and *Torquato Tasso*.

FAUST

The first part of Faust was published as a complete tragedy in 1808. The second part, which is not suitable for stage performance was published posthumously in 1833. Probably the first presentation of Faust was the W. G. Wills adaptation in 1885 for the English stage produced with much splendor and success by Sir Henry Irving.

SCENE: *Germany and imaginary realms of the nether world.*

THE learned Dr. Faust has taken for his province all knowledge. He is honored by students who come from afar; he is revered by the townspeople to whose ills he ministers. But the farther he pursues his studies the more is he convinced of the futility of man.

Mephistopheles, knowing Faust's dissatisfaction, makes a wager with the Lord that he, the Devil, can win Faust's soul. Thus it comes about that Faust in his experiments with the supernatural conjures up the Devil himself. Mephistopheles proposes that he will enable Faust to experience all the pleasures the world has to offer, providing that, if Faust shall wish to hold any passing moment for further enjoyment, in that moment he shall die and become the Devil's own. Faust readily assents and signs a written compact with a drop of blood.

The two set out to see Life and, in order that Faust may better enjoy it, visit first a witch a drink of whose brew renews Faust's youth. With renewed youth comes interest in romance and Faust demands that Mephisto procure for him the love of the innocent Margaret whom he has just seen leaving the cathedral. Margaret's purity and faith in her lover make her an easy prey for Mephisto, and she is soon the talk of the town. The gossip reaches the ears of her soldier brother, Valentine, who swears to kill her seducer. Under Mephisto's guidance, Faust, instead, kills Valentine and is forced to flee.

Too late Faust learns the awful sequel, that Margaret has been condemned to death for the murder of her mother and drowning of her babe. He insists that Mephistopheles must rescue her. The best the devil can do is to get Faust the jailer's keys. Half crazed with remorse and grief, Margaret is slow to respond to Faust's attempt at rescue. When at last Mephisto rises through the floor of the cell to bid Faust hurry, a fleeting moment of sanity reveals him to Margaret in his true likeness. Casting herself on the mercy of the Lord she bids Faust go forever.

The second part relates Faust's adventures at an emperor's court; in the underworld where he has gone in pursuit of the Grecian Helen; and in many other imaginative scenes. Gradually there is born in him the consciousness that through service to humanity one lives in the memory of mankind forever. He undertakes work for the benefit of others and thus finally comes to his supreme moment. Mephistopheles is about to claim his prey, but in that moment the angels of the Lord intervene. Faust, through the sincerity of his love for Margaret and his desire to help humanity has been the means of his own redemption.

Johann Christoph Friedrich von Schiller

..{ *Born, Marbach, Württemberg, Germany, 1759* }..
{ *Died, Weimar, Germany, 1805* }

JOHANN CHRISTOPH FRIEDRICH VON SCHILLER'S earliest dramatic effort, *The Robbers*, resulted in a prison sentence for its youthful author, when it was presented at Mannheim in 1782. Upon finishing his schooling he had been forced to take a position as army surgeon. The regiment to which he was attached was stationed near Mannheim at the time of the initial production of *The Robbers*. Having seen his first-born brain child once,

Schiller slipped away a second time to watch a performance. His absence was discovered and on his return he was sentenced to two weeks in prison and, far worse, forbidden to publish anything but medical treatises.

Although Schiller was the son of an army surgeon he had wished as a child to become a clergyman. The autocratic Duke Karl of Württemberg, however, had insisted on placing the lad in his military academy. It is small wonder, then, that as soon as possible after his prison experience Schiller contrived his release from unwelcome military service.

In 1787 came the production of *Don Carlos*. The success of this play not only brought Schiller an invitation to Weimar, the German Athens, but made his name known throughout most of Europe. About 1794 an acquaintanceship with the great Goethe ripened into one of the perfect friendships of history with a marked effect on Schiller's subsequent writings. It was with Goethe's interested advice that the *Wallenstein* trilogy was completed and produced at Weimar. This drama, a story of the Thirty Years' War, as an "acting" play has never been surpassed on the German stage. The work on it served to turn Schiller's attention definitely to historical subjects as a basis for his dramatic writing.

The *Maid of Orleans* was first performed in Leipzig in 1801. At its close the audience waited silent and bareheaded outside the theater to do its author honor. The *Bride of Messina*, a historical tragedy constructed along Greek lines, has been much admired but has never achieved the popularity accorded some of his other plays. Schiller's last finished play, *Wilhelm Tell*, is probably universally regarded as his best. It shows a sharp contrast to his preceding works. While it is tragic in intent, "success crowns a sane activity, fate yields to will and a certain serenity of spirit breathes over the whole."[1]

Sandwiched in between all these successful dramas were critical, historical and philosophical essays, as well as lyric poetry that is known today by every German school boy, the most famous being *The Song of the Bell*. Schiller, apparently at the height of his dramatic power, was at work on a Russian tragedy, titled *Demetrius*, at the time of his death in 1805.

[1]The New International Encyclopedia.

WILHELM TELL

Produced in March, 1804, probably at Weimar.

SCENE: *The Swiss mountains and a public square in a Swiss village.*

IN AN attempt to add the free and prosperous cantons of Switzerland to his ever-growing dominions, the Emperor of Austria has sent the tyrant, Gessler, to oppress the liberty-loving people. Their wives are dishonored, their oxen and herds confiscated, and the people themselves tortured and imprisoned on the slightest pretext. The crowning insult comes when Gessler has his hat affixed to a pole in the public square and insists that every Swiss man uncover and make obeisance to the hat as to the governor himself.

The patriots secretly organize against the unbearable tyranny. They agree, however, to wait a propitious moment before striking their blow for freedom. They hope in the meantime to gain the support and leadership of the young noble, Rudens. This young man has attached himself to Gessler's court on account of his love for Bertha, a Swiss noblewoman whom Gessler himself would like to marry.

Shortly after Gessler's hat has been placed in the square with two guards to enforce respect, Wilhelm Tell, famous archer and huntsman, comes down into the town accompanied by his young son, Walter. Intent on the wrongs of his countrymen, Tell starts through the square quite oblivious of both hat and guards. He is promptly seized, but as he is about to be led away Gessler and his hunting party appear. With diabolical cruelty the governor stakes the lives of both Tell and his son on the archer's ability to shoot an apple from young Walter's head at 80 paces. Tell is successful, but when the governor discovers that a second arrow would have pierced his own heart had Tell failed, he orders the archer bound and taken along.

A sudden furious squall while the governor's party is crossing the lake opens an opportunity for Tell's escape. He hides on the rim of a narrow defile through which the governor's party must pass. The governor escapes the fury of the waves, but as he rides through the pass Tell's arrow finds his heart.

The news spreads like wildfire and serves as a signal for the uprising of the Swiss patriots. Led by Rudens who has finally realized the true condition of affairs, they burn the fortresses and the governor's castle, barely managing to rescue Lady Bertha who has been imprisoned there. When all signs of Austrian tyranny lie in ruins, Rudens and Bertha pledge their lives to the leadership and protection of a free Switzerland.

Victor Marie Hugo

.{ *Born, Besancon, France, 1802* }..
{ *Died, Paris, France, 1885* }

IN A truly great dramatist the situations spring from the characters, but in Hugo's plays, as in Calderon's and Corneille's, the situation dominates the characters." This fault will be found alike in Hugo's first produced play, *Cromwell,* which appeared when its author was only twenty-five years old, and his two greatest stage successes, *Hernani* and *Ruy Blas.* The critic remarks further: "The situation in *Hernani* is strained and dramatically unreal, the sentiment is mawkish, the oratory grandiloquent; but a throbbing life and intensely ex-

pressed emotion maintain the interest, though this is a lyric rather than a dramatic one." The same might be said of *Ruy Blas.* Yet these two dramas are still played in France and go far toward explaining Hugo's contemporary popularity.

Hugo's father was an officer in the French army, and most of his early life was spent in Paris with the exception of a year in Madrid where his father's military duties had taken him. This youthful experience left its imprint both on *Hernani* and *Ruy Blas.*

Hugo's interest in literature began young. In his early teens he was already entering poetical contests and was occasionally successful. At seventeen he founded a fortnightly journal which, however, was short-lived. At nineteen he wrote a play, *Amy Robsart,* taken for the most part from Scott's *Kenilworth.* This was put aside, and when at twenty-five, his *Cromwell* was successfully produced, he did not consider it fitting that his earlier effort on a borrowed subject should appear under his own name. He gave *Amy Robsart* to his brother-in-law, Paul Foucher, but when the latter produced it anonymously it was enthusiastically hissed. The youthful Hugo promptly claimed his share of the failure, a welcome character contrast to his later years which were "devoid of humor and filled with a self-glorifying vanity."

When Hugo was twenty-eight his much fought-over *Hernani* was produced, playing for 100 nights to audiences almost equally divided between disapproving classicists and adherents of the new romanticism. His thirtieth year saw the production of *L' roi s'amuse* which later became the libretto for Verdi's opera, *Rigoletto.* A great many critics consider *Ruy Blas* which appeared in 1838 his best dramatic effort, although, if popularity be the test, the laurels must rest with *Hernani.*

When Hugo died in Paris at the age of eighty-three his funeral became a pageant any sovereign might envy. He is probably better known to posterity as the author of the lengthy novel, *Les Miserables,* than as a successful playwright.

HERNANI

*The first production of this play in Paris, February 25, 1830, precipitated a furious debate
between the adherents of romanticism and classicism that raged for months while
Hernani played to packed houses.*
SCENE: *Spain in the year 1519 A.D.*

THE lovely Dona Sol de Silva is betrothed
to her uncle and guardian, the aged Don
Ruy Gomez de Silva. Her love, however, has
been pledged to Hernani, a young outlaw.
During her uncle's absence, Dona Sol has arranged a meeting with Hernani in an upper room
of her uncle's house reached by a secret stairway.
When her duenna opens the secret door thinking
to admit Hernani, a stranger steps into the room.
He forces her to answer his questions about
Dona Sol and then to hide him in a small closet.

Shortly after Hernani's arrival, the stranger
tires of his cramped position and steps forth.
As he and Hernani are about to cross swords,
Don Ruy unexpectedly returns. The stranger is
revealed as King Charles of Spain, come under
pretense of secretly consulting Don Ruy.

King Charles has overheard Dona Sol's plan
to flee with Hernani the following night. He
contrives to arrive in advance and gives the
prearranged signal. When Dona Sol comes out
she is seized by the King, but rescued by the
timely arrival of Hernani. The latter realizes
that his defiance of the King will make him a
marked man. He refuses, therefore, to take
Dona Sol, bidding her marry her uncle, instead,
as arranged.

With his companions routed and himself
hard pressed, Hernani claims sanctuary in the
country castle of Ruy de Silva on the very day
that was to have seen the marriage of Dona
Sol. De Silva pledges his guest's safety before
he learns his identity and his love for Dona Sol.
When the King and his troops arrive in pursuit
of Hernani, Don Ruy hides him and offers his
own life instead. The King refuses and carries
off Dona Sol as hostage.

After their departure Don Ruy challenges
Hernani to a duel. Hernani refuses, saying
that his life is already forfeit to his savior.
He suggests, instead, that they both turn their
attention to the rescue of Dona Sol. As pledge
of his good faith, he gives Don Ruy his hunting
horn and swears by his father's memory that
whenever Don Ruy shall blow that horn,
Hernani will end his own life.

Meanwhile, however, King Charles is elected
German Emperor. Since personal grudges do
not befit this high position he pardons Hernani,
who is revealed as the noble Don Juan of
Aragon. As a crowning gesture of graciousness,
his Imperial Majesty bestows on his former
enemy the hand of Dona Sol. On his wedding
eve Don Juan hears the blast from his hunting
horn. When Dona Sol's pleas fail to move her
uncle to mercy, she joins her lover in death.

*Gustave Worms
as "Don Carlos"*

Kates

Alexander Dumas (Fils)

·{ *Born, Paris, 1824*
Died, Marly-le-Roi, France, 1895 }·

ALEXANDER DUMAS, the Younger, ranks as one of the three leading French dramatists of the last quarter of the 19th century. Although the theme of illicit love has always played an important part on the French stage, Dumas's obsession with the subject amounted almost to a mania. Eleven plays written before 1880 all have illicit love as the motif. Yet Dumas liked to regard himself as a moralist and teacher, a position that seems to us of the 20th century somewhat contradictory.

Perhaps a psychiatrist would find in the fact that he, like his father, was an illegitimate child, an explanation of his harping so constantly on the single theme. The torment of his school days when he was constantly taunted with his illegitimacy succeeded to a Bohemian comradeship with the father, who had publicly acknowledged his son as soon as his own literary reputation was sufficiently established to bring in a dependable income. This life eventually landed Dumas, fils, in debt to the tune of 50,000 francs. Finally, when only his pen stood between himself and disgrace, he brought forth in 1848 the famous "*Lady of the Camellias*" (known in America as *Camille*), first as a novel, then in a dramatic version. This drama, however, had to wait three years before it was finally produced in 1852. It took for its subject the sorrows of "the professional light sister," a type of play of which Hugo's *Marian Delorme* was one of the earliest representatives. Its immediate and enthusiastic reception seemed to indicate that the public was ready and waiting to sympathize with that particular type of heroine.

Dumas's second play, *Diane de Lys*, had the same subject as the first. His third play, *Le Demi-monde*, which appeared in 1855, is rated as the best of all his dramatic works. Some critics go so far as to regard it as the model of 19th century comedy. This play varies the theme of the first two somewhat "by depicting the attempts of a clever but socially discredited woman to reestablish herself in respectable society."[1]

From the day of his first dramatic success Dumas, fils, became a serious, hard-working author, and very soon an independent and wealthy one. Obviously, however, he lacked the vital and abounding genius of his writer father whose talents were given primarily to the creation of novels, and whose *Monte Cristo* and *Three Musketeers* will go down through the ages.

[1]Martha Bellinger in *A Short History of the Drama*.

LE DEMI-MONDE

(The Outer Edge of Society)

Produced on the Paris stage in 1855. The action takes place in Paris, partly at the home of Olivier and partly in that of Suzanne.

THE Baroness Suzanne D'Ange belongs to that questionable stratum of Parisian society full of married women whose husbands are never seen. She has had "affairs" with the Marquis de Thonnerins and more recently with Olivier de Jalin. Now, however, she has met the attractive young officer, Raymond de Nanjac, just back from ten years in the African service, and unacquainted with the new social development that enables women like Suzanne to live on the fringe of society. In his openly expressed admiration she sees an opportunity for marriage and social rehabilitation if she can persuade the Marquis and Olivier to keep silent.

As luck will have it, Olivier and Raymond meet and immediately become warm friends. When Olivier realizes that marriage is Raymond's intent he feels it his duty to warn his friend. Raymond is both incredulous and resentful. Suzanne, however, realizes that Olivier's words are bound to rouse her fiance's suspicions. She asks Olivier to return her letters and cleverly arranges to have Raymond meet him at her house, where she finds occasion to prove that the letters are not even in her handwriting. The certificates purporting to record her marriage to the Baron D'Ange and his subsequent death serve as final convincing proof of her innocence and complete Olivier's confusion.

Meanwhile, de Thonnerins, discovering a family friendship with de Nanjac, warns Suzanne that her marriage must not take place. She promises that it shall not, but writes the Marquis a tearful appeal to keep her secret. Raymond discovers this letter on the eve of the duel he is about to fight with Olivier in defense of Suzanne's honor. An emotional scene is followed by his offer of forgiveness providing she will return de Thonnerins's "settlement" and swear that Olivier has been nothing to her.

Since both men insist on going through with the duel which is scheduled for the grounds behind Olivier's apartment, Suzanne goes to his rooms to await its outcome. At length Olivier appears and pretends that jealousy of Suzanne has driven him to kill Raymond. Always an opportunist, the girl readily accedes to his plea that she go away with him, at which point de Jalin bursts out laughing and Raymond appears. Suzanne's final duplicity has entirely cured his infatuation, but he makes the gentlemanly gesture of offering to restore to her from his own fortune the "settlement" he had forced her to return. Seeing that she has irrevocably lost, Suzanne admits that "in her confusion" she had returned some valueless papers to de Thonnerins and so can still continue to live without Raymond's help.

Cécile Sorel of the Comédie Francaise

Björnstjerne Björnson

.·{ *Born, Kvikne, Norway, 1832* }·.
{ *Died, Paris, France, 1910* }

THE lingual root, "Björn—." of Björnstjerne Björnson's name means "bear." In disposition, however, Björnson was anything but bearlike. This contemporary, friend, and rival of the great Ibsen, was almost the direct opposite of Ibsen in every way. Ibsen preferred solitude; Björnson was what in modern slang would be termed "a good mixer." Ibsen left his native shores in disdain; Björnson stayed to work for the political and literary freedom of Norway, and for forty years was recognized as leader of the Liberal Party.

Björnstjerne Björnson was the son of a Lutheran pastor, and in his father's various pastorates passed his youth in a land rich in legendary associations. As a young man he left the University of Christiania to devote his time to journalism and in 1858 published his first drama, the one-act play, *Between the Battles.* It was also in 1858 that he was made director of the theater in Bergen. This appointment was followed in 1860 by a government stipend that enabled him to travel quite widely on the continent and thus gain the broader experience essential to a successful playwright and novelist.

Björnson's marriage to a woman trained as an actress was more fortunate than that of many playwrights, giving him a rare and lasting companionship. His friendship with Ibsen at one time suffered eclipse through a misunderstanding. The marriage of Björnson's daughter, a singer of some note, to Ibsen's son subsequently served to hold the two men more closely together.

In 1903 Björnson was given the Nobel award for literature. At this time he was probably more widely read than any other Scandinavian of his day. In fact, his translated works surpassed even those of Ibsen. Björnson wrote novels, poetry and drama almost equally well. With the exception of Ibsen in drama, he is undoubtedly the greatest literary figure Norway has thus far produced.

Björnson's early plays were lyric in their expression and decidedly romantic and religious in type. Of the dramas of this early period, *Sigurd the Bad* is probably the best known. As his interest in national politics and social problems grew, the character of Björnson's writing changed. The plays and novels of his later period are much more realistic, and frequently are even somewhat didactic in style. *A Bankruptcy,* published in 1874, and *Beyond Our Power, Part I,* published in 1883, are not only representative of this later period, but are probably the two best known of all Björnson's plays. Other problem plays, almost equally well known, are *Leonarda; The Gauntlet;* and *The Editor.*

A BANKRUPTCY

Published at Copenhagen in 1874. It soon made a success on the stages of Christiania, Bergen and Copenhagen. The first performance was actually in a Swedish translation at at Stockholm a few days before it was produced in Christiania.
SCENE: *The home of Henning Tjælde in a small seaport town.*

THE business enterprises of Henning Tjælde, merchant and brewer, provide many workers with employment; their payrolls are an important item in the commerce of the small seaport town; and their expansion from time to time furnishes Tjælde's friends and acquaintances opportunity for investment of their capital.

Tjælde's daughters, Signe and Valborg, have been brought up in the usual idleness of daughters of the rich. Signe's interest lies mainly in escaping boredom by trips to the city with her lieutenant-fiancé, while Valborg has an uncanny instinct for business and scorns the attentions of her father's confidential clerk, Sannæs.

We meet Tjælde on his return from the bankruptcy sale of his former friend Moller, by whose failure he himself has lost heavily. In the discussion of his trip, Valborg contends sympathy should go, not to Moller, but to his daughters whom he had treated most unfairly by not acquainting them with the true state of his affairs.

It appears that Tjælde's own affairs are none too stable, when Sannæs announces there is no money for the payroll due that day because the banks have suddenly shut down on loans. Almost on the heels of this news, Tjælde receives an unexpected visit from the lawyer, Berent, a bankruptcy specialist from the outside world. Berent persuades him to tender a financial statement of his enterprises ostensibly to use in judging the condition of other businesses in the community. Tjælde grossly overestimates his resources, gambling on the chance that he will gain the support of powerful Christiania financiers represented by a certain Lind whom he is expecting for dinner that afternoon. When Lind departs it would seem that Tjælde has been successful. Berent, however, returns to tell him that his financial statement is over-optimistic; that he is actually insolvent to the extent of some 40,000 pounds; and that Berent has wired Lind's firm to refuse the promised loan.

Tjælde lacks the courage to shoot Berent as he threatens to do, and finally signs the bankruptcy petition. After Berent's departure he tries to escape with some gold that Mrs. Tjælde had saved from her housekeeping allowance for just such an emergency. His escape is prevented, however, by officers on guard around the house and the gold is used to pay his laborers who are already staging a demonstration. In the end, after the departure of the receiver's men, a family united in poverty, as they never were in affluence, face the world with a fresh sense of moral cleanliness, and take up the struggle to pay off their creditors.

BEYOND OUR POWER

Although Part I of the two plays by this name was published in 1883 it was not until May 29, 1893, that it was first presented at the Théâtre Libre in Paris. The play received German production at the Berliner Theater, March 24, 1900, and was produced in New York at the Republic Theater, January 18, 1902, with Mrs. Patrick Campbell in the leading rôle.

SCENE: *Pastor Sang's house in a little Norwegian village.*

PASTOR SANG'S wife, Clara, has been bed-ridden for months. Sang's unbelievable goodness and his supreme faith in God's power have enabled him through prayer to make many miraculous cures. He has not, however, been able to cure his wife, because she lacks the faith to pray with him.

Clara's life with Sang has been an unending struggle. She has watched his comfortable fortune dwindle through his benefactions until the family is in poverty. Sang's faith that the Lord will provide is as great as ever, but it has apparently been Clara's more practical efforts in support of that faith that have brought her to her present pass. She is, to be plain, a sacrifice to her husband's divine faith.

By the greatest effort Clara has managed to give their two children an education in the outside world, hoping that thus they may escape the same sacrifice to their father's absolute faith. The children have just come home. When Sang asks them to join him in praying for their mother, they sorrowfully admit their discovery that religion is simply another compromise; that their father is the only absolutely good man in the world.

Far from blaming them, Sang blames himself that he has doubted the power of his prayers alone and unaided. He announces that he is going to the church to pray; that he will cease only when his wife sleeps and, waking refreshed, walks, cured, to meet him. Scarcely have the prayers started when Clara falls into the refreshing sleep so long denied her.

The news of the awaited miracle quickly spreads. So intense is the interest that the company on a mission ship passing by the harbor insists that the bishop put in at the village to await the miracle. The bishop and pastors are much upset. Most of them feel that it is a pity that, just as the profession of religion was becoming well ordered, one like Sang should shake it to its very foundation by encouraging the people to take God's word about faith literally.

Then the miracle happens. Clara wakes. Through their midst she walks to embrace her husband. The effort to give him this crowning miracle, however, is the final sacrifice her love can offer and she dies in his arms. Sang lays her down with an incredulous look Heavenward and murmurs: "This was not my intention." He pauses as though questioning. His own consciousness apparently answers. Whatever that answer, the shock is too great, and Pastor Sang, too, falls dead.

Henrik Ibsen

{ *Born, Skien, Norway, 1828*
Died, Christiania, Norway, 1906 }

THE principal thing is that one remain veracious and faithful in one's relation to oneself. The great thing is not to will one thing rather than another, but to will that which one is absolutely compelled to will, because one is oneself and cannot do otherwise. Anything else will drag us into deception."[1]

There, in Ibsen's own words expressed in one of his letters, is the motivating spirit breathing through the works of this great genius. Probably in all the world of drama no more solitary figure will be found. From his poverty-stricken boyhood, when he neither sought nor made friends, to his wealthy old age, when he walked the streets of Christiania with his hands always behind him or sat always alone in the same place in the same café, he lived within himself.

Perhaps his nearest approach to normal intercourse was on the occasion of his seventieth birthday. After a life of poverty spent mostly in a self-enforced exile embittered by the reception of his work in his native Norway, Ibsen had at last come back to Christiania an honored and affluent citizen. Early on the morning of his birthday, a messenger arrived bearing a silver service. This was the gift of a group of his admirers in England, "a group that included Mr. Asquith, Mr. J. M. Barrie, Mr. Thomas Hardy, Mr. Henry Arthur Jones, Mr. Pinero, and Mr. Bernard Shaw. . . . The poet's surprise and pleasure were emphatic."[2] All day long as the various delegations of important people came with their felicitations, Ibsen occupied himself with taking them up to the case where this treasure had been housed and proudly pointing it out.

Probably, too, no other dramatist ever got along with fewer contacts with the world of books. Ibsen drew the material for his plays from a keen observation of the life and reactions of the people around him coupled with his own vivid imagination.

Perhaps the most widely famous of all his plays is *A Doll's House*, although *An Enemy of the People* is considered by many critics to show greater dramatic perfection. The publication of *Ghosts* stirred an enormous amount of controversy, not only in Norway, but in other countries of the continent and in England. In many countries it might never have reached the stage except for the growth of the independent theater movement. *Hedda Gabbler* and *Rosmersholm* are probably almost as well known today as *A Doll's House*. In addition, *Pillars of Society, The Wild Duck*, the imaginative *Peer Gynt*, and *The Master Builder* are known to Ibsen lovers the world over.

[1], [2]Quotations from *Henrik Ibsen* by Edmund Gosse.

A DOLL'S HOUSE

First production, Christiania Theatre, January 20, 1880.
SCENE: *The flat of the Helmers in Christiania.*   TIME: *From Christmas Eve to Christmas Night.*

AFTER eight years of poverty the lawyer, Torwald Helmer, has been appointed manager of the Joint Stock Bank in Christiania. One of his first plans is for the replacement of a certain Krogstad, a former lawyer, who had been disbarred for forgery. In Krogstad's place Helmer plans to put Mrs. Christina Linden, a girlhood friend of his wife, Nora, and a former fiancée of Krogstad.

During the lean years Nora had borrowed money from Krogstad to save her husband's life, forging her father's signature as endorser. Through the years, while she has been struggling to pay off the loan her constant fear has been that her husband might find out that she had borrowed money. Now with his job and

respectability at stake Krogstad threatens to expose Nora to her husband unless she intercedes for him. Her intercession is, of course, quite useless, and Krogstad drops a letter in the mail box telling Helmer he will expose Nora's forgery unless he is retained at the bank.

In despair Nora consults Mrs. Linden. The latter believes she still has influence with Krogstad, so for twenty-four hectic hours Nora exerts all her wiles to keep her husband away from the mail box. On Christmas night, however, he opens it and finds the letter.

Now Helmer has always wished for dragons to slay for his lovely wife, and Nora has believed that when he learned the truth he would insist on shouldering the blame. To prevent this she has even planned to drown herself. She is, therefore, dumfounded at his submission to Krogstad's terms and his repudiation of her as his wife and the mother of their children.

Meanwhile Christina has at last seen Krogstad. They have rediscovered their love for each other and in his newborn hope and kindliness Krogstad returns Nora's note and apologizes for his threats.

With the danger to his reputation dissolved, Helmer is at once ready to forgive Nora and make her again his adored plaything. Not so Nora. Her world has been rocked on its foundations and fallen. She has discovered that love and honest intent do not count in the eyes of the world; that the man who, she thought, loved her to the point of any sacrifice, regards her merely as the plaything of his lighter hours. She resolves to leave him and her children and to learn from struggle and first-hand contact what the world she must live in is really like. The only hope she holds out for a reconciliation is that Helmer may someday become the man she had always thought him.

AN ENEMY OF THE PEOPLE

Performed early in 1883 in Norway, Sweden and Denmark; in 1893 at the Haymarket Theater, London, by Sir (then Mr.) Herbert Beerbohm Tree.

SCENE: *A small seaport town in Norway.*

IN SPITE of long absence, Dr. Thomas Stockman has always held his native town in warm regard. But one day he conceives the idea that if the supposedly health-giving properties of the water in the locality were made available through properly constructed Baths, it would not only be a boon to invalids but would also be the means of bringing prosperity to the town. He communicates his idea to his brother, Peter, who is Mayor, Chief Constable, and a generally important person. Through Peter a corporation is formed to construct the Baths. Thomas is lifted from poverty and obscurity to become the Medical Officer of the new venture. The townspeople are enthusiastic over the prospect of improved business conditions.

During the first season, Dr. Stockman notes that there is considerable illness of the typhoid variety among the visitors to the Baths. By means of chemical analysis he confirms his suspicions that the water is so badly polluted by refuse from the tanneries above the town as to be extremely dangerous. The only remedy will be to lay new conduits with a higher intake level at a cost of many thousands of pounds.

Dr. Stockman proposes to publish his findings in the "People's Messenger," whose "liberal" editor, Hovstad, is often a guest in the Stockman home and who has assured him of support in his fight for purifying the Baths. Aslaksen, the printer, who is chairman of the Householders' Association, also assures him that he will have the "compact majority" of the common people back of him. Dr. Stockman is elated.

When, however, the Mayor points out to the editor and to Aslaksen that the tax payers will have to foot the bill for the proposed changes, the former finds that he is not so revolutionary after all, and the latter, that it would be against the personal interests of the Householders' Association to support Dr. Stockman.

Since the columns of the paper and all the halls of the town are closed to him, the doctor calls a meeting in the house of his friend, Captain Horster, still believing that public opinion will be with him. Instead, the meeting denounces him as an "enemy of the people." His resignation as Medical Officer of the Baths is requested; his daughter, Petra, who has shared her father's advanced ideas, loses her job as a school teacher, and the two younger boys are forced out of school. Captain Horster, even, is "relieved" of his ship because of having loaned his house for the meeting. Dr. Stockman is at last convinced that anyone who dares to have ideas ahead of the stupidity of the masses is doomed to stand ever alone.

August Strindberg

..{ *Born, Stockholm, Sweden, 1849* }..
..{ *Died, Stockholm, Sweden, 1912* }..

AS MAETERLINCK has been called the "Belgian Shakspere," so August Strindberg is sometimes known as the "Shakspere of Sweden," because of his clear-cut and powerful characterizations. The production in 1887 of *The Father* established his reputation as one of the most powerful dramatists in Europe.

Success came to Strindberg, however, only after a youth embittered by poverty and a contentious temperament that kept him constantly in hot water with his professors at

Upsala University, until he finally left without obtaining his degree. Until friends procured for him in 1874 a post in the Royal Library at Stockholm he lived a Bohemian existence made up of school teaching, tutoring, journalism, acting, and writing. His first play, *Master Olaf*, was finished in 1872 but it was six years before he could persuade any manager to produce it. When it finally appeared on the stage in 1878, it helped to inaugurate the revolution against the old conventions in Swedish literature.

Strindberg's dramatic forte lies in the portrayal of the conflicts between human minds. The struggles in his plays are almost entirely for mental dominance. Probably no playwright in all dramatic history has expressed in his plays such bitterness toward women. The writer, Martha Bellinger,[1] says that Strindberg was subject to periodic attacks of insanity and that he suffered from an erotic mania that prevented his finding happiness or satisfaction in marriage. Certain it is that many of his plays, notably *The Countess Julia*, *The Father*, *The Link*, *Creditors*, and *Comrades*, picture woman as a complete fiend. B. H. Clark[2] believes that *Creditors* furnishes an example of the finest "mental duel" in modern drama.

In 1897, after spending more than a year in a sanitarium for mental treatment due to overwork and the painful process of one of his three divorces, Strindberg established his own Intimate Theater in Stockholm. In this he produced his own plays practically up to the time of his death.

Strindberg's work is sometimes classified in three periods: his early works which showed romanticist tendencies; the morbid realism of his middle years, when he was firmly convinced of woman's intellectual, moral, and biological inferiority; and a third and last period given over to a mysticism inspired by the example of Maeterlinck, and represented in drama by *Swanwhite*, *The Dream Play* and *Dance of Death*. His legendary play, *The Wanderings of Lucky-Per*, while not particularly characteristic, was extremely popular. In all, Strindberg is credited with 49 plays.

[1] In her *A Short History of the Drama.*
[2] In *The Continental Drama of Today.*

THE FATHER

This play which has sometimes been called the most terrible ever translated into the English language received its first production in Paris in 1887 at M. Antoine's Théâtre Libre. Productions followed at Copenhagen in 1889; October 12, 1890, at the Freie Buhne in Berlin; July 23, 1911, in London with Warner and Edith Oland; in New York at the Berkeley Theater, April, 1912.

SCENE: *The living room of a Cavalry Captain's house.*

THE married life of the Cavalry Captain and his wife, Laura, has been one constant struggle of man against woman for supremacy, and the Captain has throughout proved the weaker of the two. His wife's determination to rule has even cost him promotion in his profession. Two things he has left: his pride in their daughter, Bertha, and the knowledge that some scientific studies whose results he is nearly ready to announce will bring him fame. He is determined, come what may, that he will decide his daughter's career, but Laura is too clever for him.

She has gotten rid of the old village doctor who knew her too well and refused to lend himself to her schemes. In his place she has persuaded a Doctor Östermark to come to the village. She gets the doctor's ear before he meets her husband and plants doubts as to her husband's sanity in his mind. If she can get the Captain adjudged insane, she will be the one to decide Bertha's future. Laura's step-mother and even the Captain's old nurse, Margret, join in the unholy conspiracy of female against male.

In the opening action the Captain has had occasion to reprimand his orderly, Nöjd, for an affair with a maid in the Captain's household. Nöjd's declaration that a man can never be sure whether or not he is the father of a woman's child sticks in the Captain's mind. A chance remark of Laura's leads her husband to wonder if, after all, Bertha is his child. It suits Laura's purpose to give him no satisfaction as to the answer. While his mind is engrossed with this new worry, he learns that his wife has been intercepting both his outgoing and incoming mail regarding his scientific discoveries. Because of the resulting delay, the Germans who have also been working along similar lines, will be able to forestall his announcement.

His chance to establish his own personality in the world is gone. If Bertha is not his daughter, then he can no longer look forward to projecting his personality through her. It is too much for the Captain to contemplate and the insanity his wife has been pretending comes upon him. His one expressed regret is that Laura could not have retained toward him the mother instinct. With the awakening of sex love, he explains, come inevitable enmity and strife . . . the war for supremacy that can only end in complete defeat for one or the other.

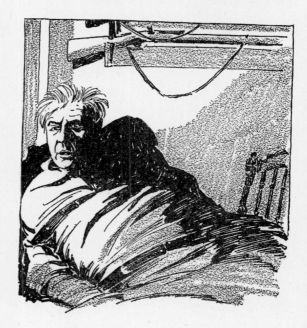

Alexander Pushkin

.·{ *Born, Moscow, 1799*
Died St. Petersburg, 1837 }·.

IN A sense Alexander Pushkin is the beginning of real Russian drama. With his first play, *Boris Godunov* (written in 1825), he broke, or perhaps we should say, established, several precedents. First of all, his plot was chosen from a somewhat legendary incident of Russian history. His characters were real Russians, thinking, speaking, living as Russians. Instead of following French or German examples, as writers for the stage had done heretofore, he experimented with romantic tragedy after the style of Shakspere. As a reading play, *Boris*

is, in spots, superb; as an acting play it leaves much to be desired, and as a matter of fact did not reach production. Its influence on later dramatic writers was considerable, however.

Alexander Pushkin on his father's side was descended from one of the oldest families of the Russian gentry. His mother was the grand-daughter of Peter the Great's Abyssinian Engineer-General. The young Alexander's first poems appeared when he was but fifteen, and by the time he left school he was regarded as a rival by the acknowledged literary leaders of the day.

After Pushkin left school, he lived a riotous life in St. Petersburg as a member of the most brilliant and dissipated crowd in the capital. Seditious utterances in certain of his writings caused his banishment from St. Petersburg, and finally what was almost an incarceration on his mother's estate. When somewhat later he was pardoned and permitted to return to the capital, he found that under the pretense of favoring him the Czar was in reality curtailing both his personal and literary liberty. When later on he was appointed to a court position simply so that the Czar could invite his beautiful wife to the court balls, Pushkin's bitterness knew no bounds. He was powerless to change the situation, however, and in 1837 challenged one of his wife's admirers to a duel which resulted in the writer's death.

Pushkin's greatest contemporary successes with the general public were his two poems, *The Captive of the Caucasus* and *The Fountain of Bakhchisaray*, and the drama, *Boris Godunov*. Viewed from a critical angle, however, his real masterpieces are the poem, *The Bronze Horseman*, and the drama, *The Stone Guest*, which concerns itself with the closing love intrigue and tragic ending of the Spanish Don Juan.

It has been left for later generations of Russians to appreciate Pushkin's true worth. It is significant that he was practically the only writer of pre-Revolutionary Russia who escaped the general condemnation of the Bolsheviks of everything that smacked of aristocratic culture.

BORIS GODUNOV

This play was written in 1825, but for political reasons was refused production.

SCENE: *Various localities in Russia and Poland.* TIME: *1598–1605.*

IVAN, THE TERRIBLE, was followed on the Russian throne by his weak-minded son, Feodor. This necessitated the establishment of a Regency to which the already powerful noble, Boris Godunov, was appointed. Not satisfied with being the virtual ruler of Russia, Boris contrived the death of Feodor's younger brother, Dimitri, and in due time, actually succeeded in making himself Czar of Russia.

For several years Boris sat more or less securely on the Russian throne. But gradually whispers of the true fate of Dimitri began to be noised about, and at last reached the ears of an ambitious young monk named Gregory. This young man immediately realized that the murdered Dimitri would have been practically the same age as himself. He knew, too, that the Poles were only waiting for an excuse to cross the Russian frontier in an aggressive war. So he decided to risk his life and fortune on a bold impersonation of the slain Prince and a claim to the Russian throne, knowing full well that Boris Godunov would not dare produce proofs of the boy's death.

Biding his time, he managed to escape from the monastery. Successfully eluding pursuit, he crossed the frontier and presented himself and his claims to the leaders of the Polish nobility, who, as he had foreseen, received him with open arms. So it came about that in a short space of time, the Pretender, Gregory, at the head of a large and powerful Polish army, invaded Russia intent on establishing his fraudulent claim to the Russian throne.

Meanwhile a whole series of disasters had been plaguing Boris Godunov. Famine and pestilence had stripped the land. His throne, never too secure, had been made less so by the incessant plotting of the nobles against him. Worst of all, advancing age and the continuous struggles had weakened Boris, both in mind and will. When the news was brought to him that the Pretender was actually on Russian soil and advancing toward the Russian capital, a vision of the murdered Prince arose before him and he realized that the time of retribution was at hand.

For an old man so weakened in mind and body, the supposed reappearance of the slain boy was too great a shock. There in the council chamber in the presence of his nobles he swooned and, conscience-stricken and contrite, died while the army of the Pretender was still far from the Russian capital.

Anton Chekhov

{ *Born 1860, Tagenrog, Russia*
Died 1904, Badenweiler, Germany **}**

IF ONE is to read or see Chekhov's plays with interest or understanding he must remember that "there is no subject matter in Chekhov's plays, no plot, no action."[1] They consist of a mass of atmospheric detail placed almost invariably around the underlying theme of the mutual lack of understanding among human beings. "Russian realistic drama," it must be remembered "is essentially static."[2]

Yet the man who evidenced so great an originality in drama and literature that no compatriot has been able successfully to imitate him, was the grandson of an almost unlettered serf. Through a certain cleverness in trading, this grandfather was enabled to save up money enough to buy his own freedom and that of his family. His son Pavel, or Paul, also had a shrewdness that served him well in the store he opened in Tagenrog. The family prospered until a new railroad, passing Tagenrog by, went through a rival village. This eventually destroyed the elder Chekhov's business and reduced the family to poverty.

Finally all the family except young Anton moved to Moscow. He remained behind "tutoring" for his board and room for three years until he completed the course at the local "high school." After that he matriculated at the University of Moscow with the intention of becoming a doctor. Faced from the first with the need not only of supporting himself but of helping with the family support, he began to contribute stories to a weekly comic paper. It is by these stories, which English and American opinion would consider unspeakably vulgar, that Chekov is known to the great multitude of Russians today. The stories and plays of his maturity, which in translation brought him world fame, are known to a comparatively small circle of Russian "intelligentsia."

Chekhov, the man, was a gregarious soul. He wanted people always about him and his house was constantly overrun with guests. Most of his life was lived in the shadow of tuberculosis. Physician, though he was, he refused to take the proper care of himself. He finally succumbed to the ravages of the disease at the prime of his dramatic power, just six months after the outstandingly successful presentation of *The Cherry Orchard*. Three other Chekhov dramas rank among English-speaking peoples almost on a par with *The Cherry Orchard*. They are *The Sea Gull*, *Uncle Vanya* and *The Three Sisters*.

[1], [2] Prince D. S. Mirsky in *Contemporary Russian Literature*.

THE CHERRY ORCHARD

Produced at the Moscow Art Theater, January 30, 1904.

SCENE: *The family estate of Madame Ranevsky.* TIME: *Spring.*

MADAME RANEVSKY and her daughter, Anya, return from Paris to find that their family estate is about to be sold at auction for debt. To all the family it is quite unthinkable that they should lose the wonderful cherry orchard whose white blooms are part of their childhood memories. Madame Ranevsky is an irresponsible soul who cannot be made to realize the value of money. Her brother, Gayef, is quite as hopeless where money is concerned. Barbara, the step-daughter, is the only practical one, but how can a woman raise money?

Lopahkin, a former serf, has become a wealthy landowner. Out of his admiration for Madame Ranevsky and a genuine affection that remains from childhood days, he suggests that if they will tear down the house and raze the cherry orchard, they can cut the property up into the popular new villa sites. The entire property, he assures them, will promptly be leased and the substantial income it will afford, will enable them to live where and as they please.

Family pride combined with a spirit of procrastination prevents their accepting this suggestion even if their fondness for their cherry orchard would permit their considering its destruction. They continue to believe that some miracle will save their orchard. Thus they drift along until the day set for the sale. Grandmother has sent them fifteen hundred pounds and Madame Ranevsky and her brother feel sure this will serve to redeem the place. When Gayef and Lopahkin return from the sale, however, it is to report that Gayef's paltry sum has been ludicrously insufficient. Lopahkin has bought the place and is full of an immense satisfaction at owning the estate where his grandfather and father had once been slaves.

Now that the inevitable has happened, the various members of the family readjust themselves surprisingly well. Madame Ranevsky prepares to return to Paris to live on the fifteen hundred pounds; Gayef takes a job in the bank; Barbara, a position as housekeeper. Peter, the former tutor and "perpetual student," prepares to return to his beloved university. Even young Anya looks forward to taking her independent place in the world. So they separate . . . each one intent on his own future. At the last, with characteristic inefficiency, they lock the old manservant, Firs, in the house, believing that he has already been sent to the hospital. The only sound as the curtain falls is the ringing of axes in the cherry orchard.

OTHER RUSSIAN DRAMATISTS

Alexander Griboyedov	(1795–1829)	A. F. Pisemsky	(1820–1881)
Nikolai Gogol	(1809–1852)	Leo Tolstoi	(1828–1910)
A. N. Ostrovsky	(1823–1886)	Maxim Gorky	(1868–)
Alexei Tolstoi	(1817–1875)	Leonid Andreyev	(1871–1919)

CONTEMPORARY with Pushkin was Alexander Griboyedov. He is remembered for his one great comedy, *Woe from Wit*, or as it is sometimes translated, *The Misfortune of Being Clever*. This play belongs to the school of classical comedy and is reminiscent of Molière for sparkling dialogue and keen characterization. The plot, however, is of secondary importance.

Following Griboyedov by a few years, Nikolai Gogol produced two brilliant satires, both entirely Russian in theme and characterization. The first of these, *Revisor* (*The Inspector-General*), is rated by many critics as the greatest play in the Russian language. New Yorkers had the opportunity to see it revived on the stage in 1934 by the visiting players from the Moscow

"The Power of Darkness" by Leo Tolstoi

Art Theater. Gogol's second comedy, *Marriage*, is almost equally good.

A. N. Ostrovsky, the great dramatist of the Russian realistic theater, is sometimes called the creator of modern Russian drama. The first production of an Ostrovsky play in 1853 "inaugurated a new theatrical era that lasted for half a century."[1] From 1853 on, not a year passed that did not see a new Ostrovsky play on the stage. Griboyedov and Gogol probably had greater genius than Ostrovsky, but the latter left a lasting monument to his efforts by the creation of a school of Russian drama and a truly national Russian theater. Of all his plays the comedy, *Poverty Is No Crime*, received the most contemporary popular applause. *The Thunderstorm*, a later tragedy, is, however, rated as his masterpiece, and *The Forest* shares in its critical acclaim.

It was not until 1860 that Russian drama remembered the initial impulse given by *Boris Godunov* to the creation of historical plays. About that time a flood of plays in blank verse, based on incidents of Russian history, began to appear. Most of them were entirely unimportant, but Alexei Tolstoi produced a work of lasting fame in his historical trilogy consisting of *Ivan the Terrible*, *Tsar Theodore*, and *Tsar Boris*. Realistic tragedy toward the turn of the century is represented by Pisemsky's *A Hard Lot* and by Leo Tolstoi's *Powers of Darkness*. The latter play was written when Tolstoi had passed middle age and had become more or less of a religious fanatic. It is really more of a Morality than a true tragic drama. Gorky's *Night Asylum* (also known as *In the Depths*) and *He Who Gets Slapped*, a tragi-comedy by Leonid Andreyev, have achieved success outside of Russia. Thus we fit these lesser Russian dramatists into their particular niches in the evolution of Russian drama from the great Pushkin to the modern Chekhov.

[1] Prince D. S. Mirsky in *A History of Russian Literature*.

PLAYS OUR GRANDFATHERS ENJOYED

WITH the death in 1890 of the Irish actor-playwright, Dion Boucicault, the American stage became more completely native than ever before. Boucicault's place as manager of the Madison Square Theater was filled by an American playwright from the midwest, Augustus Thomas, and thereafter foreign plays or American plays fashioned on foreign patterns became increasingly rare.

It is true, of course, that for ten years or more such playwrights as James A. Herne had been writing dramas with a substantially American background. Among these were *Hearts of Oak* (1879), *Sag Harbor* (1900) and *Shore Acres*, which proved a favorite with theater-goers in those closing years of the nineteenth century. Then there was *The Old Homestead* by Denman Thompson . . . and *Hazel Kirke* by Steele Mackaye, both of which helped to establish an American tradition. *Hazel Kirke*, in fact, ran two years in New York, sent ten companies on the road, and appeared for some thirty years in stock company productions.

Bronson Howard is generally regarded as the transition link between drama of the nineteenth century and that of the twentieth. He was born in Detroit, wrote for the *New York Tribune* and *Evening Post*, and finally reached the stage in the rôle of playwright. *Shenandoah*, a Civil War drama, *The Young Mrs. Winthrop*, *The Henrietta*, and *Saratoga* were all widely acclaimed successes of the final thirty years of the past century. Barrett H. Clark in his *Theories of the Modern Drama* declares: "Howard deserves the title of 'Dean of American Drama' because he was the first to awaken to the fact that in the America of his day there was material for an indigenous drama, and he did his best in spite of French influences, to throw off the conventions of the past and point a way to the future." In our day, however, it is customary to award the honorary title of "Dean" to Augustus Thomas who up to his death in August, 1934, continued to take a lively interest though not an active part in the affairs of Broadway.

At the turn of the century two dramatists who wrote most successfully were: Clyde Fitch with such plays as *Beau Brummel, The Truth, The Climbers, The Girl with the Green Eyes;* and *The City;* and William Gillette with his Civil War dramas, *Secret Service* and *Held by the Enemy.* Fitch's first and most successful play, *Beau Brummel*, was enacted by Richard Mansfield, who claimed also to have had a large share in writing it.

Charles A. Hoyt, who died in 1900, was a prolific writer of native American comedies that in type were forerunners of the modern musical comedy revue, among them: *A Bunch of Keys, A Rag Baby, A Texas Steer, A Milkwhite Flag,* and any number of others all beginning with the magic "A." These were the days, too, of that Paul Kester who wrote *When Knighthood Was in Flower* for Julia Marlowe, and of George Broadhurst whose success reached its peak in *Bought and Paid For.* But already we overlap and must give way for the playwrights of a new century.

Maurice Maeterlinck

..{ *Born, Ghent, Belgium, 1862* }..

THE year 1889 saw the production of three "first" plays by playwrights who were shortly to become famous. These budding dramatists were Gerhart Hauptmann and Hermann Sudermann of Germany, and Count Maurice Maeterlinck who is sometimes called the "Belgian Shakespere."

In appearance Maeterlinck is the direct opposite of the mysticism of his writings. The word that best describes him would be "hearty." Nor does the brilliant success of his plays seem to have affected the playwright's personality. According to one of his commentators,[1] he appeared frank, modest and sincere when he visited America for the first time in 1919. Unfortunately the lecture he had specially prepared for the opening of his lecture tour was couched in such original terms that it left the public, his most ardent admirers included, quite at sea.

Maeterlinck was born of a very old Flemish family. He was educated at the College of Sainte-Barbe and later studied law at Ghent. Shortly after finishing his schooling he settled in Paris where he made the acquaintance of the leaders of the symbolist school of French poetry. These contacts combined with his own deeply religious instincts are probably largely responsible for the characteristics of Maeterlinck's earlier plays. Almost without exception these are occupied with the spiritual adventures of souls, and refuse to be bound by the ordinary facts of time and space.

His career as a writer began in 1889 with a volume of verse and, as has been said, his first play, *The Princess Maleine*. Three years later, in 1892, the well-known *Pelléas and Mélisande* appeared. The critics, William Lyon Phelps and Ludwig Lewisohn, agree that three short plays—*L'Intruse*, *Les Aveugles*, and *Intérieur*, are the best of his earlier works.

Maeterlinck's later plays, represented particularly by *Monna Vanna* and *Mary Magdalene*, are in decided contrast to the tendencies of the earlier ones, while *The Bluebird*, the Christmas novelty by which he is best known in America, is an imaginative play in a class by itself. *Monna Vanna*, his first brilliant success was played on every important stage in Europe except in England where it was forbidden by the censor. *Sister Beatrice*, of the later period, has been rated by Phelps as one of the best acting plays of the 20th century. The title rôle of this play was sympathetically interpreted in America by Edith Wynne Mathison.

In 1911 the playwright was honored with the Nobel Prize for literary achievement.

[1] Wm. Lyon Phelps in his *Essays on Modern Dramatists*.

THE BLUEBIRD

Initial performance at the Moscow Art Theater, September 30, 1908. First American production, New Theater, New York, October 1, 1910.

SCENE: *The humble cottage of the Tyls; the land of imagination.*

AT THE behest of the Fairy Berylune the the brother and sister, Tyltyl and Mytyl, set out on Christmas Eve to look for the Blue Bird of Happiness to cure the Fairy's little daughter who is ill. Before they leave the Tyl cottage the Fairy gives Tyltyl a little green hat to wear. She tells him that when he turns the diamond in the front of the hat it will release the Souls both of Animals and of Things so that the children can converse with them. At once Tyltyl tries it out and the children are promptly surrounded with a babel of voices from the Dog, the Cat, Milk, Fire, Water, Sugar, Bread and Light. So boisterous is their celebration of their release that Daddy Tyl is heard stirring in his bed in the next room. At this Tyltyl turns the diamond back so suddenly that none of the souls have time to get back into their everyday guise, and have no choice but to accompany the children on their search. All but the Dog are much upset by this, for if the children are successful their companions will have to die at the end of the journey.

The Fairy pilots them all out through the window just as Daddy Tyl opens the door and reports to Mummy Tyl that the children are sleeping peacefully. When they arrive at the Fairy's castle, each one is permitted to choose a costume from a huge chest. The Cat, on the sly, organizes all the Things into a conspiracy to prevent the children's success, except the Dog and Light who are frankly on the children's side.

The group set out on their quest. In the Land of Memory they enjoy a visit with Granny and Gaffir Tyl and the children's little dead brothers and sisters. Thereafter they visit the Palace of Night, the Forest, the Palace of Happiness, the Graveyard, and the Kingdom of the Future. Several times they think they have found the Blue Bird but on reaching the light of day it has turned pink or black or has died.

Finally, on Christmas morning in their own home, the children discover that their own turtle dove is blue. When Neighbor Berlingot begs the bird for her sick daughter they make a willing gift of it and the child is miraculously cured. But such is the transitory nature of happiness that the Blue Bird is no sooner found than it flies away and the search must begin again.

Fire   Bread   Sugar   Milk   Tylette, the Cat   Tyle, the Dog   Light

Henry Arthur Jones

Born, Grandborough, England, 1851
Died, Hampstead, England, 1929

THE circumstances surrounding the early life of Henry Arthur Jones would generally be considered anything but favorable to a successful dramatic career. He was the son of a Buckinghamshire farmer. What education he received was brief and acquired in a local grammar school. At 13 he went "into business" and was a commercial traveller until he was 30. The people among whom he was raised believed that drama was the invention of the devil and that those who went to the theater were bound straight for perdition. If Jones became a dramatist it was because the urge within him was so strong he couldn't help it. His first play was written when he was 16, two years before he ever saw the inside of a theater. His first produced play, *Only Round the Corner*, was staged in 1878. The melodrama, *The Silver King*, written in collaboration with Henry Herman and produced in 1882, assured his position as a dramatist.

Henry Arthur Jones belongs to that period sometimes referred to as the "Victorian Transition." It was the period when drama was trying to free itself from its inherited superficialities and to become a part of contemporary life. In 1884, Jones made an attempt at serious drama in his *Saints and Sinners*. It was hooted by the first-night audience and condemned by the press. Discouraged Jones returned to melodrama.

In 1896, when London had become to a certain extent "Isben-conscious," Jones made another attempt at serious drama with *Michael and His Lost Angel*. Again he was hooted by the audience and condemned by the critics. It was too forward looking for that generation and not sufficiently plain spoken for the next, as a later attempt at a revival proved. In the opinion of Jones himself and of some of his commentators it deserves to be rated as his best effort. The following year, however, he returned to the polite, superficial type of comedy with *The Liars*, following it in 1900 with *Mrs. Dane's Defense*. *The Lie* had its première in New York in 1914 and did not reach the London stage until 1923. There even so capable an actress as Sybil Thorndike, could not save it from vitriolic comment from the pen of the renowned English dramatic critic, James Agate.

Henry Arthur Jones made a start with the new dramatic movement. He was never able, however, to shake off the influence of that early Victorian period when his work began, nor to achieve a real success with the newer trend of dramatic thought.

THE LIARS

Produced in London in 1897.

SCENE: *Freddie Tatton's house in the Thames valley; a private sitting room at an inn; Lady Rosamund's house in London; Sir Christopher's London flat.*

LADY JESSICA NEPEAN is fond of flirtation, not so much because she is dissatisfied with her husband, Gilbert, as because it flatters her vanity to keep other men dangling just on the edge of a proposal. At the houseparty of her sister, Lady Rosamund Tatton, her flirtation with Edward Falkner, a recently returned South African hero, is the theme of conversation. Everyone insists that Sir Christopher Deering who had stood sponsor for Falkner socially must reason him out of his infatuation for Lady Jessica before her husband realizes what is occurring. The women of the party also attempt to reason with Lady Jessica.

Both attempts, however, are foredoomed. Falkner is desperately in love with Lady Jessica, as only a lonely and serious man can be. Lady Jessica is enjoying his ardor immensely, and still believes she can end it with a word. Business calls Gilbert Nepean away, so when the houseparty breaks up Lady Jessica keeps an appointment to have dinner with Falkner at the inn where he is staying. Her husband's brother, George accidentally comes upon her there and, putting the worst possible construction on it, feels himself bound to wire Gilbert to return at once.

Lady Jessica happens to see Rosamund and Freddie rowing down the river, and manages to get her sister into the inn. In hopes to forestall George they write Gilbert a letter asking him to call at Lady Rosamund's town house the next morning for an explanation. About the time Gilbert is due, most of the other members of the houseparty turn up at Lady Rosamund's on some pretext or other. When Gilbert arrives, he is met with a most amazing barrage of lies. To complicate the situation, he has already seen a member of the houseparty on his way from the station, and

by a chance remark of hers, recognizes these subsequent explanations as lies.

Finally when Lady Jessica sees that they are hopelessly involved, she bids Falkner tell the truth. By this time she imagines herself as much in love with him as he with her and is ready to run away with him.

Sir Christopher, however, is determined that his friend shall not sacrifice a brilliant career for a shallow woman. He manages to reconcile Lady Jessica and her husband by the simple process of blaming Gilbert for the whole affair. "In future," Sir Christopher advises, "flirt with your wife yourself if you don't want some other man to do it."

Conway Tearle and Grace George

Sir Arthur Wing Pinero

..{Born, London, 1855}..
..{Died, London, 1934}..

"THERE will be some trouble about 'biography' because I have never troubled myself to supply particulars of my early life to any writer."[1] The quotation is from a letter written by Sir Arthur to that able and friendly commentator, Clayton Hamilton. Nevertheless, we know the things that are most interesting: that his practice in writing was, not to conceive a theme and fit his characters to its exposition, but rather to gather together in his mind a group of everyday characters and watch their reactions to each other; that, when not absorbed in writing a play he was the friendliest of men; and, finally, that it was his achievements in the field of drama that in 1909 were recognized with knighthood.

Arthur Wing Pinero was in race, part Jew and part Gentile; in blood, part Latin and part Anglo-Saxon; in name, Portuguese. His father was a solicitor and he himself was educated for the law. He preferred, however, at 19, to get himself a job as an actor and made connection with the theater in Edinburgh at the munificent salary of one pound a week. Two years later he arrived at the Globe Theater, London, and it was not a great while before he saw a brief one-act play of his performed as a "curtain raiser." The success of that and subsequent short plays emboldened him to give up acting and to devote his time to dramatic writing.

His fortune and contemporary fame were secured by that sentimental success, *Sweet Lavender*, and the very playable farce, *The Magistrate*. His enduring fame, if he be so fortunate, will very probably rest on *The Second Mrs. Tanqueray*. Following its production in 1893 there were other serious plays . . . *Trelawney of the Wells, The Notorious Mrs. Ebbsmith, Iris, The Thunderbolt* and *Midchannel*. None of these, however, was accorded the public acclaim which greeted *The Second Mrs. Tanqueray*.

It was Sir Arthur's custom to direct all rehearsals and literally train each actor in the interpretation of his or her part, but such was his shyness that nothing could persuade him to attend "first nights." He had made one visit to America in the eighteen eighties to direct the rehearsals of *The Magistrate*. When, in 1910, he was urged by Mr. Hamilton to make a second visit, he replied:

"I'd like to see America but I'm afraid to risk it. As soon as I got over Mr. Frohman might request me to sit in a box at the performance of one of my plays."

[1] Quoted in Clayton Hamilton's Introduction to an edition of Pinero's *Social Plays*.

THE SECOND MRS. TANQUERAY

Initial performance May 27, 1893, at the St. James Theater, London, with Mrs. Patrick Campbell as Paula.

SCENE: *Aubrey Tanqueray's bachelor flat in London on the eve of his second marriage; the Tanqueray home at Willowmere, Surrey, a few months later.*

ON THE eve of his second marriage Aubrey Tanqueray entertains his three closest masculine friends at dinner. He makes it in the nature of a farewell, for, as he succinctly puts it, married friends' wives frequently don't find each other congenial. In response to their questions as to whom he is to marry, he answers: "After tomorrow she will be Mrs. Aubrey Tanqueray."

His bachelor friend, Cayley Drummle, remains after the others leave and to him Aubrey confesses that he is marrying a certain "Mrs." Jarman, a woman with a "past." Shortly after Drummle, too, has gone, Paula Jarman herself arrives bringing Aubrey a letter confessing certain details of her past, a letter which he chivalrously burns unopened. After Paula's departure, Aubrey reads the letter from his convent-reared daughter which until now he has had no chance to open. It announces that his daughter has changed her mind and is coming to live with him.

A few months later finds Mr. and Mrs. Aubrey Tanqueray "at home" at Willowmere, Surrey, together with the seventeen-year-old Ellean. The situation is tense. The neighbors, although old friends of Aubrey's, have conspicuously refrained from calling. Ellean, too, senses something in Paula that repels her, while Paula is jealously anxious to win Ellean's confidence and friendship.

Finally Paula insists that since the neighbors will have none of them she is going to invite Lord George Orreyed and his chorus girl wife to be their guests. Horrified, Aubrey persuades her not to mail her letter of invitation. At this point their nearest neighbor does call but only to get permission to take Ellean to Paris and later to London for the season. When Aubrey gives this permission, admitting that they themselves cannot give Ellean the social background to which she is entitled, Paula defiantly mails her letter to the Orreyeds.

Paula finds herself badly bored with her guests, but refuses to make up with her husband. This is the situation when Ellean returns to ask her father's permission for her engagement to a Captain Ardale. Paula feels impelled to confess to Aubrey that the man who now wants to marry his daughter had been her lover. Ellean with uncanny instinct divines the situation and taunts Paula with the sort of "past" that she has already condoned in Ardale. In a final realization that for a woman with a "past" there can be no future, Paula kills herself.

"Yes," wails Ellean, "Yes, so everybody will say. But I know—I helped kill her. If I'd only been merciful!"

MRS. PATRICK CAMPBELL
as *Paula Tanqueray*

Oscar Wilde

..{ *Born, Dublin, Ireland, 1854* }..
   { *Died, Paris, France, 1900* }

AFTER the first performance of *Lady Windermere's Fan*, Clemence Scott, veteran nineteenth century critic of London drama, wrote in *The Daily Telegraph:* "The play is a bad one but it will succeed. No faults of construction, no failure in interest, no feebleness in motive, will weigh in the scale against the insolence of its caricature."

This criticism sums up the spirit of the playwright himself. He thumbed his nose, so to

speak, at the world. In his college days he delighted to scorn what were referred to as the "manly sports," thereby earning a reputation for effeminacy. He decorated his rooms with all sorts of "artistic" impedimenta. In fact, his general attitude got him a ducking at Oxford where he went from Trinity College, Dublin.

Oscar Fingall O'Flahertie Wills Wilde was the son of a famous Irish surgeon. His mother was a graceful writer of verse and prose, and it was doubtless to her early influence that Wilde owed his interest in literature. After he left college he became interested in "art for art's sake," and became sufficiently prominent to be invited to lecture in the United States.

Wilde had written considerable verse, fairy stories, and other prose, and had made some attempt at drama before the successful production of *Lady Windermere's Fan* in 1892. This was followed by *A Woman of No Importance* (1893), *An Ideal Husband* (1895), and *The Importance of Being Earnest* (also 1895). This was his last play and the only one that received favorable notice from the press.

It was shortly after the production of this play that Wilde brought the notorious libel suit against the Marquis of Queensbury. The revelations of the trial were such that Wilde was sentenced to two years' imprisonment with hard labor. Out of this experience came his famous *Ballad of Reading Gaol.* He came out of prison, however, broken in body and spirit. For the brief remainder of his life he lived on the continent under the name of "Sebastian Melmoth."

Wilde's play, *Salome*, written in French in 1893 for Sarah Bernhardt, received a single performance in Paris in 1904, and is today much better known through Richard Strauss's operetta, for which it served as the libretto. Wilde's plays, whether good or bad dramatically, are gifted with a theatrical effectiveness and a brilliance of wit and epigram that easily account for whatever success they enjoyed. *The Importance of Being Earnest*, his first serious drama, might have spelled the beginning of a worthwhile dramatic achievement. Who knows?

The IMPORTANCE of BEING EARNEST

Produced at the St. James Theater, London, February 14, 1895.

SCENE: *The London flat of Algernon Moncrieff and the country estate of Jack Worthing.*

JACK WORTHING, who lives in the country, pretends to have a younger brother, Ernest, whose escapades frequently call Jack to London. Algernon Moncrieff pretends to have an invalid friend, "Bunbury," whose attacks call Algernon into the country whenever there is a distasteful social function in prospect. This activity Algernon refers to as "Bunburying."

Jack has managed to hide from Algernon the location of his country place and the existence of an attractive ward, Cecily Cardew. In Algernon's bachelor flat at the tea hour, Jack confesses he has come to town to propose to Algernon's cousin, Gwendolyn, who knows him as "Ernest." Algernon refuses his help unless Jack explains the inscription on his cigarette case which Algernon has found. Thus Cecily's existence is revealed, but Jack stubbornly refuses to reveal her whereabouts.

Gwendolyn accepts Jack, confessing she has always felt that a man named "Ernest" was her fate. During a subsequent catechism by Gwendolyn's mother, Lady Bracknell, Jack gives his country address which Algernon takes down with the intention of going "Bunburying" during Jack's absence from home. When Lady Bracknell learns that Jack's identity dates from the discovery of a baby in a large black handbag in Victoria station she refuses consent for the marriage.

Cecily, alone in the country with her governess, Miss Prism, is agreeably surprised at the appearance of Algernon in the guise of the much-discussed "Ernest." The young couple lose no time in becoming engaged for, Cecily admits, the name "Ernest" has always fascinated her. When Jack returns unexpectedly to announce "Ernest's" sudden death in Paris, he is disagreeably surprised to learn that "Ernest" is at the very moment in the house.

While Jack and Algernon are separately arranging with the rector for a rechristening, Gwendolyn arrives. The discovery of Gwendolyn and Cecily that they both seem to be engaged to "Ernest Worthing" results in a strained situation. The appearance of both young men clarifies the matter of engagements, but also reveals that neither is named "Ernest." When the girls learn that their fiancés had been about to be rechristened for their sakes, they forgive the deception.

With the arrival of Lady Bracknell the question of consent again comes up. Lady Bracknell is quite willing that Algernon shall marry Cecily and her fortune. Jack, however, as Cecily's guardian, refuses his consent unless Lady Bracknell permits his marriage to Gwendolyn. The appearance of Miss Prism who is recognized by Lady Bracknell, results in the identification of Jack Worthing as Algernon's lost elder brother, Ernest, thus settling matters to everyone's satisfaction.

Edmond Rostand

{ *Born, Marseilles, France, 1869* }
{ *Died, Southern France, 1918* }

WHEREVER a translation of the famous *Cyrano de Bergerac* exists, the lasting fame of the French poet-dramatist Edmond Rostand is assured. In fact, all three of his best known plays . . . *Cyrano*, *L'Aiglon*, and *Le Chanticler* . . . stand alone in the roster of romantic plays. The gorgeous rhythm of the poetry, for example, in *Cyrano*; the sheer audacity of a most unusual hero; and, finally, the beauty of the sentiment place this play in a class by itself with the best of Sophocles, Shakspere or Molière.

Rostand's father was a brilliant and wealthy journalist. Young Rostand was educated in Paris and, like so many men of his day and class, studied law and received his degree. His mind, however, had been set from boyhood for writing plays.

In 1890, when Rostand was only 22, he published a volume of poems, his first work of any note. In 1894 his first important play, *The Romancers*, was produced at the Comédie Française. If proof were needed that his contemporaries considered him a successful playwright, the fact that the great Bernhardt played the following year in his *The Faraway Princess*, and again in 1897 in *The Woman of Samaria* would be sufficient.

The greatest rôle in any of Rostand's plays, Cyrano, was planned and written especially for the great French actor, Constant Coquelin. It was at the actor's request, in fact, that the final death scene was planned. All of Rostand's best works, it seems, are tragedies, yet they leave the audience with a feeling of happiness and inspiration that many a comedy fails of producing. As one critic has it: "Death in Rostand is more cheerful than Life in Maeterlinck."[1]

When, in 1901, following the success of *L'Aiglon*, Rostand was elected to the French Academy, he was the youngest member ever chosen for that honor. The hold that Rostand secured on a far-flung audience cannot be better illustrated than by an incident that occurred on the occasion of the first performance of *Chanticler* in Paris. On the following day, "a daily newspaper in Butte, Montana, devoted, not the first column, but the entire first page to *Chanticler!*"[2]

Rostand was prevented from living in Paris by his delicate health which required a kinder climate. Incidentally, he could not take a walk on Paris streets without being followed by adoring crowds. He built himself a huge château at Cambo in the Pyrenees where he lived and wrote until his death in 1918. His wife, too, was a poet, who doubtless would have been famous had not her husband's star so far eclipsed her own.

[1] Quoted by William Lyon Phelps in his *Essays on Modern Dramatists* without the original source.
[2] William Lyon Phelps in his *Essays on Modern Dramatists*.

CYRANO de BERGERAC

Produced December 28, 1897, at the Théâtre de la Porte Saint-Martin, Paris, with Constant Coquelin in the title rôle. American production October 3, 1898, in the Garden Theater, New York City, with Richard Mansfield as Cyrano.

SCENE: *Paris; the siege of Arras; Paris again.*

CYRANO DE BERGERAC, guardsman and poet, is cursed with an enormous, bulbous, blossoming beak of a nose. To compensate for his fixed belief that no woman can ever love him on account of this affliction, he has made himself renowned in Paris for his personal bravery and the charm of his verse.

Cyrano's beautiful and wealthy cousin, Roxane, is much sought after. When, after a spectacular duel with a man who has been annoying her, Cyrano receives an urgent message from Roxane, he is encouraged to believe that she may actually love him. He finds, however, that she imagines herself in love with the handsome Christian de Neuvillette, newly enlisted brother guardsman in the company of Captain de Castel-Jaloux, and wants Cyrano to bring them together.

Putting aside his own love, Cyrano offers his powers of expression to Christian to assist in winning Roxane. Cyrano's eloquence in the many letters signed by Christian's name and the feeling in his voice as he declares his love under Roxane's balcony one dark night, bring about the marriage of Christian and Roxane just a few minutes before the company is ordered away to the siege of Arras.

Although their company is outnumbered, starving, and facing almost certain death, Roxane daily receives a letter signed with Christian's name. Irresistibly drawn by these letters, Roxane dares to drive through the enemies' lines to reach her Christian's side. When Christian sees the power that another's letters have had over Roxane he suddenly realizes that it is Cyrano and not himself that she really loves. He insists that Cyrano shall tell her the truth and leaves the scene. Before Cyrano has divulged the secret, however, Christian is carried in mortally wounded. When Cyrano whispers in his ear: "I have told her; it is you she loves," Christian dies happy.

After Christian's death Roxane goes to live in a convent and for some fifteen years it has been Cyrano's custom to call each Saturday afternoon on the stroke of three. In spite of innummerable enemies and abject poverty his gay invincible spirit shines forth at these meetings. Then one Saturday as he proceeds to his call, an enemy pushes a log from a window causing it to fall onto his head, breaking his skull. He hides his injury from Roxane, but begs to be allowed to read Christian's last letter which she carries always next to her heart. Only when in the gathering darkness he reads it through unfalteringly does Roxane realize that he was the writer and that through all the years it has been Cyrano that she loved.

Walter Hampden as "Cyrano"

Hermann Sudermann

.·{ *Born, Matzicken, East Prussia, 1857* }·.
    Died, Berlin, Germany, 1928

THE year 1889 saw the opening of the realistic movement in Germany. It also brought to the stage a "first" play, entitled *Die Ehre* (*Honor*) whose young author until then had been merely an obscure tutor and journalist. *Honor* proved itself an exception to most first plays in that it brought its author immediate European fame and an assured literary position. Hermann Sudermann was the son of a Men-

nonite brewer. During Sudermann's childhood his father was reasonably prosperous, but financial reverses caused the boy to be apprenticed to a chemist when he was 14. He managed to finish his studies at the gymnasium, however, and later went on to the University of Königsberg.

Sudermann had published three novels before the play, *Honor*, appeared. They lacked beauty and emotional power, but revealed a keen observation and a sure dramatic instinct. Probably few playwrights have had their work subjected to more bitter controversy. When *Honor* was first produced it was widely acclaimed, only to be just as enthusiastically denounced at a later date. Because of the popular and financial success of his plays, Sudermann has been frequently accused of writing for the box office.

Almost as soon as his literary success was assured, Sudermann married an authoress and gave himself up entirely to writing. He belonged, however, to the realistic school of the last quarter of the 19th century and could not adapt himself successfully to the post-war literary outlook. He continued to write, however, right up to his death, his last play appearing in 1925 and his last novel in 1928.

Probably the best known of Sudermann's plays is *Die Heimat*, translated under the title, *Magda*, the name of its heroine. The powerful title rôle of this play has attracted such capable actresses as Modjeska, Bernhardt, Duse, and Mrs. Patrick Campbell. This fact in itself has doubtless contributed largely to the play's success. A morose play, *The Destruction of Sodom*, a comedy quite out of his usual style, *The Battle of the Butterflies*, *The Vale of Content*, *St. John's Fires*, *Storm-Brother Socrates* and *The Joy of Living* are among the better known of his plays. *Dame Care*, *Regina*, and *The Song of Songs* are the best known of his novels so far as English readers are concerned. Sudermann had little of the poetic beauty that characterizes the dramatic works of his famous contemporary, Hauptmann, but he was by instinct a man of the theater and a true dramatist. For nearly a quarter of a century the names Sudermann and Hauptmann, dominated the German stage.

DIE HEIMAT

(The Home . . . Played in America as "Magda")

First production at the Lessing-Theater, Berlin, January 7, 1893.

SCENE: *The principal city of a German province.* TIME: *Contemporary.*

TEN years before the opening of the play, Magda, elder daughter of Lieutenant-Colonel Schwartz, retired, left home rather than submit to her father's dictation and marry Pastor Heffterdingt. Thereafter the mention of her name is forbidden in the house and nothing is known of her subsequent life. At the opening of the play she is discovered to be the famous Wagnerian prima donna, Maddalene dall'Orto, guest star of the impending music festival in the town. Heffterdingt, who for ten years has blamed himself for the rift between Magda and her family, uses all his persuasiveness to bring about a reconciliation between Magda and her father. Finally, against her better judgment, Magda consents to spend the night under her father's roof.

Among the first callers the following morning is the ambitious Councillor von Keller. Magda recognizes him at once as the man she had loved those first few wretched months away from home . . . the man who had promptly faded from her life and left her to bear his child alone and uncared for. Now that she is famous, he is anxious to pick up the old acquaintance. Magda, however, is through with him . . . with all men. There are in her whole life but two things . . . her son and her music.

Von Keller's call and Magda's subsequent pallor and distraction arouse Schwartz's ever-ready suspicions, and he pries the truth from her. When he challenges von Keller to a duel the latter counters with a proposal of marriage to Magda. Because of her love and pity for her father, Magda finally consents. When she finds, however, that von Keller's proposal does not include recognition of his son, she withdraws her consent. Her father, outraged by his

daughter's viewpoint, locks her up in a room with him and announces that neither of them will leave it alive unless she promises him that she will marry Councillor von Keller and rehabilitate the family honor. Magda can see only one possibility of saving their lives and still retaining that personal freedom more precious to her than life itself.

"How can you be sure," she asks her father, "that he was the only man in my life?"

As the significance of Magda's question dawns on him he raises his gun to shoot her. But the shock has been too great for his enfeebled system, and a stroke of apoplexy stays his hand and ends his life.

Gerhart Hauptmann

..·{ *Born, Obersalsbrunn, Silesia, 1862* }··

GERHART HAUPTMANN is another of that trio of European dramatists who made their stage début in 1889. Hauptmann's first play, *Before Sunrise*, was produced in that year at the German Free Theater, and was acknowledged as the beginning of an important new literary movement for Germany just as Strindberg's *Master Olaf* had been recognized as the beginning of Swedish literary independence.

Hauptmann's dramatic genius is incontestable, but he has never seemed able to settle on any one form as best suited to express his dramatic intentions. *The Weavers*, for example, a play that caused considerable stir on its presentation in 1892, is most unusual in that it is concerned with a whole community and has neither hero nor heroine. *The Sunken Bell*, on the other hand, is centered around one man's struggle for expression. In *Michael Kramer* it is two men who hold the center of interest.

Gerhart Hauptmann's father was a Silesian innkeeper and the boy was originally intended for a farmer. His instincts, however, were artistic rather than agricultural. After two years of study in a school of art, a year of more general education at the University of Jena, and considerable continental travel, he settled down in Rome as a sculptor. Regard for health soon brought him back to the more bracing climate of Germany, and there, after some hesitation, he gave up art for a literary career.

At the time Hauptmann's *Before Sunrise* appeared, cultivated Germans had apparently forgotten the greatness of Germany's own Goethe and Schiller and Lessing. They read only French, Russian and Scandinavian authors. In spite of a recognition of its importance, the acceptance, therefore, of Hauptmann's first play was by no means universal. He persisted, however, with other realistic plays including *Drayman Henschel*, *Lonely Lives*, and, most notable, *The Weavers*. By 1910 he had the satisfaction of seeing the German realistic movement fully established.

But realism alone did not satisfy Hauptmann's artistic cravings. In 1893 he turned to romanticism with the dream-play, *Hannele*, and followed it in 1897 by a "study in artistic temperament"[1] called *The Sunken Bell*. This play is without doubt Hauptmann's best-known work, although not his most representative one.

Some critics regard drama as Hauptmann's least happy choice in the form of literary expression. Many consider him as one of the finest poets of modern times. He has also written many well-known novels of which *Atlantis*, appearing in 1912, is probably the most famous. That, incidentally, was the year that brought Hauptmann the Nobel prize for literary achievement.

[1] Barrett H. Clark in *The Continental Drama of Today*.

THE SUNKEN BELL

Initial production December 2, 1896, at the Deutsches Theater, Berlin. American production April 29, 1897, in German at the Irving Place Theater by Frau Agnes Sorma; in English, December 21, 1899, at the Hollis Street Theater, Boston, by Sothern.

SCENE: *The mountains above the valley; the cottage of Heinrich, the bell-founder in the valley.*

HEINRICH, the famous bell-founder, has one ambition . . . to make a bell clear-toned and perfect, worthy to ring out from the little church on top the mountain for all the world to hear. When at last success seems attained, he sets out with the bell on a strong wagon drawn by eight horses. The Pastor, the Baker, the School Master, and a crowd of villagers follow on foot to assist at the hanging of the precious bell. Halfway up the mountain a wagon wheel breaks, plunging Heinrich and his precious bell deep into the abyss. The bell by reason of its great weight rolls down to the depths of the lake. Heinrich's fall, however, is broken by trees, so that at last he stumbles, bruised and semi-conscious, upon the cottage of Wittikin, the witch.

Her beautiful elfin foster-daughter, Rautendelein, wants to claim Heinrich for her own, but is prevented from doing so by the arrival of the Pastor, the Baker, and the School Master, who bear him tenderly down to his cottage in the valley. To Heinrich's devoted wife, Magda, the fate of the bell matters little "if he, the master, be but safe." Heinrich, however, reads in his misfortune a sign from Heaven that his supreme effort is considered unworthy, and he has no desire to recover from his injuries.

As he hovers between life and death, Rautendelein comes in the guise of a simple maid from the inn. She inspires him to believe that in the freer atmosphere of the mountains he can yet achieve the perfect bell. Leaving his family, he goes up into the mountains with Rautendelein. There, with the grudging help of the little mountain people, a wonderful new bell takes form. Heinrich refuses all pleas of his former neighbors and, when they try to force

him to leave the mountains and Rautendelein's inspiration, puts them to rout.

What his friends fail to accomplish, however, is achieved by the phantom forms of his two children bearing a pitcher filled with their mother's tears. Even as they speak, the tones of the sunken bell, tolled by her dead hands, rise to snatch Heinrich from victory on the heights back to his failures of the valley, while Rautendelein at last consents to wed the Nickelmann, spirit of all waters.

The call of his unfinished masterpeice, however, is too strong for Heinrich. Attempting to regain the heights and final achievement, he sells his life for one last look at Rautendelein whose inspiration had made possible the perfect, though unfinished, bell.

George Bernard Shaw

..{ *Born, Dublin, Ireland, 1856* }..

THE first published work of the noted satirist, George Bernard Shaw, was inspired by the American "revival" team, Moody and Sankey. Young Shaw attended one of their revival services in Dublin, and on his return home was moved to write a letter to *Public Opinion* in which he remarked that "if this sort of thing is religion, then I am an atheist."

Shaw was the son of a financially impractical father and a remarkable mother whose musical talent not only helped out the family income but provided young George with an excellent musical background. In his regular schooling which ended when he was fifteen, Shaw was generally near the bottom of the class. When Shaw was fifteen a friend secured him a position in the office of a Dublin land agent where he endured the drudgery of routine and figures for five years.

At twenty he followed his mother to London where she had set up as a music teacher and joined the ranks of unpublished novelists with five novels that nobody would buy. During the first nine years of his London sojourn, Shaw's literary efforts brought him something like $30 and an ardent interest in the socialistic theories that fill most of his subsequent plays.

Shaw was first acted on the stage of the Royalty Theater, London, in 1892, but created not even a little ripple. He continued his efforts with *Widower's Houses* and *Mrs. Warren's Profession*, which latter play was refused London production by the censor. His first success came when, on September 17, 1894, *Arms and the Man*, a strictly realistic comedy was presented by Richard Mansfield at the Herald Square Theater, New York. From that point on, Shaw's rise to popularity, both on the American and German stages, was steady and swift. He was not, however, conclusively accepted in the English theater until 1904.

Candida written in 1894 won a decisive success on the German stage with Frau Edith Sorma. London would have none of it, and in America Richard Mansfield lacked the courage to produce it even after he had gone so far as to put it into rehearsal. It was left for Arnold Daly to make theatrical history with his production of *Candida* in the season of 1903–4, thus marking the real beginning of the Shaw vogue.

Man and Superman was the success of the season of 1904–5 both in London and New York. In spite of Shaw's many subsequent plays, these remain his outstanding successes. Critics and public alike were cold to his latest play, *Simpleton of the Unexpected Isles*, which was an offering of a recent New York season.

ARMS AND THE MAN

Presented April 21, 1894, at the Avenue Theater, London; September 17, 1894, at the Herald Square Theater, New York, with Richard Mansfield in the title rôle; December 8, 1904, at the Deutsches Theater, Berlin, under the title "Helden."

SCENE: *The home of Major Petkoff in a Bulgarian town.*

THE Bulgarian army officered by Russians of impeccable military training has just routed a regiment of the Serbian army officered by Austrians who know war tactics equally well. Young Major Sergius Saranoff is the temporary hero because he knew no better than to lead a cavalry charge against a company of machine gunners. That his men escaped total annihilation was only because the enemy had been supplied with the wrong ammunition.

During the helter-skelter retreat of the routed regiment, Captain Bluntschli, a seasoned Swiss officer in Serbian uniform, climbs the water pipe and seeks refuge in the bedroom of Raina Petkoff, fiancée of the windmill-tilting Major Saranoff. Bluntschli insures Raina's silence with an unloaded revolver, confessing later that experienced soldiers always carry chocolate in place of ammunition. He so enlists her interest that she hides him when soldiers search the room. The next morning she and her mother send him away, his uniform hidden under an old coat of Major Petkoff's. In the pocket Raina has tucked her picture with the inscription: "To my chocolate cream soldier."

The war over, Major Petkoff and Sergius return. At every opportunity Sergius flirts with Raina's maid, Louka. Louka, who has ambitions beyond her station, confides to Sergius that his engagement would be off were the Swiss Captain to return. At this point Captain Bluntschli does come back to return the coat. He is hailed as a friend by Major Petkoff, whose wife has prevented his discovering the story of the coat, and proceeds to help the Major with some puzzling army duties.

As they finish the work, a message arrives for Bluntschli announcing his father's death and his immediate recall to Switzerland to take charge of the family's large chain of hotels. Louka has at last very cleverly maneuvered Sergius into an engagement with her. Now Bluntschli discovers that Raina is 23 instead of the 17 he had supposed, and asks for her hand. Her mother proudly informs him that she has been engaged to a man who keeps twenty horses; that the daughter of so wealthy a family as the Petkoffs could scarcely marry a man with less. "Oh, if it comes to a question of establishments," says Bluntschli, and begins to enumerate: "200 horses; 70 carriages; 4000 tablecloths," until he quite overawes Madame Petkoff. In the end Raina admits that she has fallen in love with her "chocolate soldier."

CANDIDA

Produced in 1894 by Frau Sorma on the German stage; produced December 9, 1903, at the Princess Theater, New York, and again on April 26, 1904, at the Court Theater, New York.

SCENE: *The combination library-study of the Rev. James Mavor Morell.*

JAMES MAVOR MORELL is a Socialist clergyman of the Church of England. He radiates success, happiness, force, wherever he speaks . . . and his life is filled with meetings . . . people throng to hear him. They hang on his words . . . and return to an unaltered life. Morell thoroughly believes in himself and his MISSION in life. He believes, too, that above all things he hates hypocrisy. This, in fact, is the root of his dislike for his father-in-law, Burgess. Burgess is an ignorant but successful manufacturer, the foundation of whose modest fortune rests on the starvation wages formerly paid his workers. Now he would lay claim to being a model employer and comes to make up his quarrel with Morell, who answers:

"As long as you come here honestly, as a self-respecting, thoroughly convinced scoundrel, justifying your scoundrelism and proud of it, you are welcome. But I won't have you here sniveling about being a model employer and a converted man when you're only an apostate with your coat turned for the sake of a County Council contract."

Into this scene Morell's wife, Candida returns from three weeks in the country. She has been squired from the station by Eugene March-banks, an eighteen-year-old aristocrat, who is taking his adolescence hard and quite naturally has fallen in love with the very attractive Candida. His quarrel with Morell, to whom he confesses his passion for Candida, is the same as Morell's with Burgess. When Morell would make light of his feelings with a flow of beautiful words, Marchbank exclaims: "Is it like this for her here always? Do you think a woman's soul can live on your talent for preaching?"

Candida explains to Marchbanks that Morell's mother and sisters always shielded him and that she has "carried on."

"When there is money to give, he gives it; when there is money to refuse, I refuse it. I build a castle of comfort and indulgence and love for him, and stand sentinel always to keep the little vulgar cares out."

Morell in a sudden access of humility agrees.

But Marchbanks no longer needs Candida to choose between them. Through her he has learned what love means . . . the love of the strong man for the woman he would protect against the world. Eighteen that morning, he goes out into the night "old as the world itself" . . . a man.

MAN AND SUPERMAN

Published in 1893. Produced at the Hudson Theater, New York, September 4, 1905. In stage performances Act III which is devoted to long speeches expressing Shavian theories of the relationship of the sexes is left out.

SCENE: *England; later the continent.*

JACK TANNER, an ardent and wealthy young socialist, is opposed to marriage as a matter of principle. It not only distracts man's attention from the worthwhile work of the world, but it makes him a mere appendage to woman's procreative desires. Owing to Jack's revolutionary theories, Roebuck Ramsden, who had himself been a man of "advanced ideas" some thirty years before, detests Jack as thoroughly as Jack detests the thought of marriage. It is, therefore, a matter of surprise and exasperation to these two men to find themselves named in the will of their friend, Mr. Whitefield, lately deceased, as joint guardians of his daughters, Anne and Rhoda. They would doubtless have been still more surprised could they have known that the affair was Anne's doing.

As it is, Tanner believes Anne is bent on marrying his friend, Octavius Robinson. His warnings to that young gentleman fall on barren ground, however, for marriage with Anne is Octavius's idea of Heaven. Nor does Octavius's sister, Violet, share Tanner's theories. When it seems that she is about to become a mother with no visible husband, Tanner defends her right to have her own child. Whereat this self-sufficient young woman furiously turns on him with the statement that she is a respectable married woman, even if she does decline to reveal her husband's name.

It is left for Tanner's chauffeur, a young man of great perspicacity, to apprise Tanner of the fact that he, rather than Octavius, is Anne's real quarry. The dismayed Tanner climbs into his car and tells the chauffeur to break all records reaching the continent. The capable Anne promptly arranges a motor party to pursue Tanner. Beside Ramsden and Anne's mother and sister, Octavius and Violet are included, as well as Hector Malone, a young American. The latter insists on paying Violet marked attention even though he has been confidentially told by the others that she is already married.

The motor party overtakes the runaway in the Pyrenees where he had spent the night as the enforced guest of bandits. Later, in Italy, a note from Violet, delivered by mistake to Hector Malone, Senior, reveals the young American as the missing husband, while Tanner, of course, capitulates to marriage with Anne. Defiant to the last, however, he warns everyone that all silly wedding gifts will be sold and the proceeds devoted to distributing copies of his "Revolutionists' Handbook."

Robert Loraine at Hudson Theatre, 1905

Kates

Sir James M. Barrie

··{ *Born, Kirriemuir, Scotland, 1860* }··

IN A generation given over to "realism" and "problem" plays the whimsical humor and graceful sentiment of a J. M. Barrie are as refreshing as a spring zephyr. Of all the plays of a more than usually successful playwright, Barrie's *Peter Pan*, endeared to American audiences through the charm of Maude Adams, is the most whimsical.

The boy Barrie had begun to write even before he went to school. Before he had been graduated from Edinburgh University he had almost finished a three volume novel, although there seems to have been no talk of publishing it. He landed himself a job as leader-writer on the *Nottingham Journal* in 1883, and in 1884 the article that really began his writing career appeared in a London paper, the *St. James Gazette*. Encouraged by the complimentary comments of the editor he moved to London, and in 1887 his first book, *Better Dead*, appeared. He continued to write novels and stories until 1893 when his first play, *Walker, London*, was produced.

The immediate success of the play not only added to the laurels his other writing had already brought him, but seemed to indicate that drama, rather than novels, was his true métier. Just ten years later, in 1903, he had the gratifying experience of having three successful plays running concurrently in London. They were: *Quality Street, The Admirable Crichton,* and *Little Mary*. In 1904 came *Peter Pan* of whose fantastic world Barrie's public had had a fore glimpse in 1902 in the story, *The Little White Bird*. Now in almost every nursery in London liniment was much in demand to soothe the hurts of the confident youngsters who like *Wendy* had attempted to fly. For this very reason Barrie takes care in a later printed edition of the play to warn children that before they can fly it is necessary to have some of *Peter Pan's* "fairy dust" sprinkled on them.

In 1905 came *Alice-Sit-by-the-Fire*, and in 1908 the famous *What Every Woman Knows*. *The Twelve Pound Look*, made famous in America by the genius of Ethel Barrymore, is probably the best of his one-act plays. *A Kiss for Cinderella* is a revival of the genius evidenced in 1903–4, while in 1917 came *Dear Brutus*, a fantastic dream play dedicated to the proposition that the events of our lives are fore-ordained. Barrie is at present reported to be working on a play for that fascinating German star of *Escape Me Never*, Elizabeth Bergner.

PETER PAN

*Staged in London in 1904 and later played most successfully in America by Maude Adams
and in a recent revival by Marilyn Miller.*

SCENE: *The nursery of the Darling family; the Never-Never Land.*

AS A matter of necessary economy the third floor nursery of the Darlings is guarded by Nana, a huge Newfoundland dog. On the evening of our adventures, however, Nana, in disgrace, has been shut away from her charges, Wendy, John, and Baby Michael. Consequently there in no one to prevent the entrance of Peter Pan and the fairy, Tinker Bell, when they come to retrieve Peter's shadow separated from him one day when he hovered too close to the window listening to Mrs. Darling's stories.

Tink finds the shadow but Peter has difficulty attaching it. Wendy from her bed watches with interest, and presently offers to sew it on. With this propitious start their acquaintance progresses. Wendy learns that the first laugh of every new baby becomes a fairy; also, that everytime a child says: "I don't believe in fairies," a fairy drops dead.

Presently to the infinite disgust of Tink, Peter suggests that Wendy fly away with him to Never-Never Land and become a mother to the little lost boys for whom he is Captain. Wendy consents if he will teach Michael and John to fly, too. The fairy dust that Peter blows on them enables the children with a little practice to fly well enough, so that presently they set off in Peter's wake on the exciting trip to Never-Never Land.

Here the lost children live under the ground in a house whose entrances are hollow trees. They are constantly in danger of capture by fierce pirates under the leadership of Captain Hook. Already Peter has deprived the Captain of an arm which he has thrown to a crocodile, and now the crocodile constantly follows the Captain in hopes of getting another bite. So far Hook has escaped because the ticking of a clock which the crocodile has swallowed gives warning of his approach. When the lost boys are not fighting the pirates they entertain themselves by trying to catch mermaids in the lagoon.

At length Captain Hook captures Wendy and the others. Peter comes to the rescue and Captain Hook, following his inglorious defeat, throws himself to the waiting crocodile. At last Peter flies back with the children to their despairing parents. Mrs. Darling naturally refuses to let Wendy return with Peter, proposing instead that she adopt him. That youngster, however, has no intention of going to school and growing up to work in an office. He says good-bye to Wendy and flies away over the tree tops to remain forever the "boy who never grew up."

CURLY JOHN NAPOLEON DARLING   NIBS   PETER PAN   MICHAEL NICHOLAS DARLING
TOOTLES SLIGHTLY   WENDY MOIRA DARLING   1ST TWIN
2nd TWIN

Augustus Thomas

..{   *Born, St. Louis, Missouri, 1857*
Died, Nyack, New York, 1934   }..

THERE is a superstition among some dramatic writers that a play's success is assured if only the title begins with "A." Augustus Thomas must have known of this superstition, when in 1883, following his success with a one-act adaptation of Francis Hodgson Burnett's story, *Editha's Burglar*, he wrote four other short plays: *A Leaf from the Woods; A Man of the World; A Studio Picture;* and *A New Year's Call.*

Augustus Thomas was a St. Louis newspaper man turned actor. His connection with newspaper and stage was preceded by service as a page boy both in the Missouri legislature and in Congress, and by several years of work in railway freight offices. Eventually reporting and other newspaper activities led to part ownership in a St. Louis newspaper and the gradual conviction that writing, dramatic writing, was his forte.

His short play, *A Man of the World*, had been played on tour with some success. In 1889 an elaboration of the earlier one-act arrangement of *Editha's Burglar* attracted sufficient notice to bring him in 1890 the offer of the post at the Madison Square Theater left vacant by the death of the Irish actor-playwright, Dion Boucicault. Here in 1891 *Alabama*, the first of a long series of "state" plays was produced. *Alabama*, dedicated to the cause of removing the sectional prejudice and hatred following in the wake of the Civil War, enjoyed a prompt success, and from that time on Thomas was one of the most prolific and successful American playwrights.

Other successes include: *The Hoosier Doctor; Arizona* (both produced in 1898); *Oliver Goldsmith* (1900); *The Earl of Pawtucket* (1903); *Mrs. Leffingwell's Boots* (1905); *As a Man Thinks; Copperhead* with Lionel Barrymore's superb performance; and *The Witching Hour* (1907). Of them all, the last named was probably the most outstanding. Thomas was one of the early apostles of the cult of timeliness in the matter of play production. It is reported that he wrote *The Witching Hour*, which deals with the subject of telepathy, ten years before he felt that the time was ripe for producing it.

In 1890 Thomas married a sister of former Secretary of State Bainbridge Colby. From his advent to New York in 1890 Thomas maintained an enthusiastic interest in the doings of Broadway right up to his death in August, 1934.

THE WITCHING HOUR

This play had its tryout in Providence, R.I., November 16, 1907, and its first New York performance at the Hackett Theater, November 18, with John Mason in the rôle of Jack Brookfield.

SCENE: *Jack Brookfield's gambling house in a Kentucky town; Justice Prentice's study in Washington, D. C.*

AN UNCANNY knowledge of the cards held by opposing players is the basis of Jack Brookfield's wealth. It also was the cause some twenty years before of his losing his sweetheart. Now when her son, Clay Whipple, takes to frequenting Jack's high-class gambling establishment this same mysterious ability at cards enables Jack to discourage Clay's taste for gambling by seeing to it that he always loses. Clay, however, continues to frequent the house because of Jack's niece, Viola.

Frank Hardmuth, assistant district attorney and an ambitious and unscrupulous politician, also wants to marry Viola. Hardmuth counts on Jack's backing because he has tipped Jack off to certain planned raids and otherwise connived at the breaking of laws he had sworn to enforce. For this very reason Jack considers him unsuitable and even hints that Hardmuth was involved in the recent assassination of the governor-elect.

A midnight call from Supreme Court Justice Prentice accidentally introduces Jack to the subject of telepathy and suggests an explanation of his unusual luck at cards. His consideration of this new angle is interrupted by the crowd of young people from the billiard room. Tom Denning, a half-drunk sportsman, is pursuing young Clay with a cat's eye scarf pin, for which Clay exhibits an uncontrollable aversion. Blindly he strikes out at his tormentor and accidentally kills him.

Frank Hardmuth is delighted to secure a conviction of murder in the first degree. The Supreme Court is about to decide the appeal when discovery of an old letter reveals that fear of the cat's eye jewel is hereditary in Clay's family and two generations previous had been the cause of a duel. A most irregular midnight call on Justice Prentice in Washington

is instrumental in securing a new trial on the basis of fresh evidence.

During the new trial Jack attempts to influence the jury's verdict through telepathy. He has also given to the papers the facts about the governor elect's assassination. By the time Clay is exonerated Hardmuth is in hiding. Yet in spite of his knowledge of Hardmuth's guilt, Jack helps him to escape over the state line. So convinced has he become of the power of thought that he feels he will never be sure that his own idle speculations on the possibility of an assassination had not put the plan into Hardmuth's mind.

With Clay's freedom and the closing of Jack's gambling house there is nothing to prevent the happy culmination of both romances.

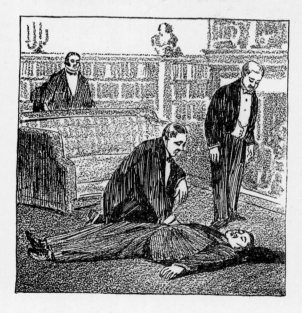

William Vaughn Moody

··{ *Born, Spencer, Indiana, 1869*
Died, Colorado Springs, Colorado, 1910 }··

WHEN William Vaughn Moody's *The Great Divide* was produced in New York in 1906 it was for a time hailed as the great American drama. It not only enjoyed success on this side of the Atlantic, but was played in London as representative of life in the great open spaces of western America.

Reading the play today, it is hard to realize that so crude a representation of life, whether eastern or western, could have passed either for truth or good drama; and that a play so unskillfully constructed and poor in characterization could have achieved the success accredited to *The Great Divide*. Perhaps the real reason was that Easterners, particularly New Yorkers, are so hazy about any sort of life west of Pittsburgh that they credulously accept almost anything as "truthful representation."

The play reaches its climax in the middle of the first act and from then on the author is hard put to it to hold the interest until the curtain drops on the final scene. *The Great Divide*, however, deserves mention in that it blazed the way for plays that used something other than the conventional "drawing room" settings and characters from middle and upper class life.

Moody's parents died while he was still a boy. He worked his way through prep school and later through Harvard University. There he acted as assistant in English during 1894–5. In 1895 he received an appointment as an instructor at the University of Chicago, and in 1901 was promoted to an assistant professorship which he held until 1903. In 1902 he collaborated in a book, *A First View of English and American Literature*, but this sort of writing was drudgery and done only that he might gain money to help his family to better things.

Moody's real interest lay in poetry. His three poetic dramas . . . *The Masque of Judgment* (1900), *The Fire Bringer* (1904), and *The Death of Eve* (incomplete at the author's death) . . . entitle him to a high place in American literature. All three are notable for richness of rhythm and a fine lyric sense. Moody's one other produced play, *The Faith Healer* (1909) attracted some attention but was not a dramatic success. It is possible, however, that had he not been cut off in his prime, Moody might have attained real success as a playwright.

THE GREAT DIVIDE

First production, October 3, 1906, at the Princess Theater, New York, with Margaret Anglin; London production, September 25, 1909, at the Adelphi Theater with Edith Wynne Mathison.

SCENE: *A cabin on the edge of an Arizona canyon; the ancestral home of the Jordans in Boston.*

RUTH JORDAN and her brother, Phil, have invested what little remains of her mother's wealth in a ranch in southern Arizona. One night when she is unavoidably left alone three half drunk men force their way into the cabin. They are about to throw dice for possession of the girl, when she appeals to the most likely looking of the lot to save her, promising in return to marry him and go away with him that night.

Stephen Ghent buys off the Mexican with a string of gold nuggets and shoots it out with "Shorty," the remaining claimant. Ruth leaves a note indicating that she has gone of her own free will with the man of her choice. She asks them not to search for her. Ruth and Steve are married by a justice and go to his prospector's cabin high up on the rim of the canyon.

During the months that follow Steve becomes half-owner of one of the fabulously rich mines in the West. He arranges to build a wonderful house as a surprise for Ruth. She, meanwhile, has been weaving baskets and making rugs which she sells to tourists at the hotel. By this means she is earning money enough to buy back the string of nuggets which her husband had paid for her.

She is seen at the hotel and recognized by Phil, Polly, his wife, and a friend, Winthrop Newbury. When they seek her out she pretends perfect happiness and claims the weaving is merely her hobby. She shows them the plans for the new house and Steve believes that at last she has really capitulated. As soon as the others go, however, her coldness returns. She asks Steve to let her buy back her freedom with the nuggets she has finally redeemed, not for her own sake but so that the child that is

about to be born can be brought up in the more suitable atmosphere of Boston.

Steve consents, but he secretly follows her to Boston at the risk of being cheated out of his half of the mine. In Boston he wins over Mrs. Jordan and Polly, perhaps by saving the homestead from foreclosure. At last they reveal his presence to Ruth. After considerable internal struggle her love for Steve conquers her feeling that they should both do penance for the unconventional circumstances of their marriage. She is finally convinced that it is only the last remnants of her Puritan heritage that have been fighting her desire for happiness, and that Steve has been right from the beginning.

Wm. Butler Yeats

..{ *Born, Dublin, Ireland, 1865* }..

WHEN Yeats's dramatic poem, *The Countess Cathleen*, was used in 1899 as the inaugural piece of the newly conceived Irish literary theater, "a politician, a cardinal, and a newspaper combined forces to stir up opposition to the play on the ground that it was blasphemous and unpatriotic."[1]   As a consequence, the opening performance was attended by a large body of Dublin police prepared to quell any disturbance.

Far from dampening the enthusiasm of the little band who were striving to create for Ireland a national theater, it spurred them on to greater efforts.   It is largely due to the leadership and vision of W. B. Yeats and Lady Augusta Gregory that we owe later successes of dramatists like Padriac Colum, J. M. Synge, "A. E." (George Russell), and the contemporary Sean O'Casey.   In the Abbey Theater under the sponsorship of the Irish National Theater Society, these playwrights found a group of sympathetic actors preëminently fitted to interpret Irish dramas many of which were destined for a lasting fame outside of Ireland.

"If frequent production be the test of popularity," says Ernest Boyd,[2] "then *The Land of Heart's Desire* is Yeats's most successful appeal to the playgoer."   This was not only Yeats's first produced play (London, 1894) but it served also to introduce him in 1901 to the American stage.

The most intensely dramatic play Yeats has written is the little one-act play titled *Cathleen ni Houlihan*.   This was Yeats's first prose dramatic work, and strangely enough, it succeeded in pleasing even the critics who had attacked his other plays with so much bitterness.   The immediate inspiration of the play, Yeats attributed to a dream, but the central figure is that ageless, legendary *Cathleen ni Houlihan* that represents Ireland herself.   The play in its finished version breathed a spirit of patriotism intense enough to satisfy the most ardent Irish Nationalist.

His modern Morality, *The Hour Glass*, performed in 1913, served as a sort of transition to Yeats's later poetic plays based on Irish legend . . . this, in spite of the fact that its first production was in prose.   Following *The Hour Glass*, a series of legendary dramas appeared: *The Shadowy Waters, On Baile's Strand, The King's Threshold, Deirdre*, and *The Green Helmet*, all of which were produced with varying success.   It is probable, however, that posterity will remember and honor Yeats more for his efforts toward building an Irish National Theater than for his dramatic contributions to that theater.

[1] Ernest A. Boyd in *The Contemporary Drama of Ireland.*
[2] In his *The Contemporary Drama of Ireland.*

THE LAND OF HEART'S DESIRE

Produced at the Avenue Theater, London, in 1894.

SCENE: *The kitchen in the cottage of Maurteen and Bridget Bruin.*

ACCORDING to ancient legend the fairies on Midsummer Eve possess a strange, unusual power over mortals. On this night they sometimes even steal away the fairest of the mortals to become their brides. It is with her head full of such fancies that Mary comes to the peasant home of Shawn Bruin as his bride. She can see no harm in the tales of the fairy folk. Indeed, she is far more interested in reading a book of legends she has found than in performing the housewifely tasks suitable to her new state. Shawn's parents, Bridget and Maurteen, appeal to Father Hart, who has come on Midsummer Eve to sup with them, to dissuade Mary from her book. She is, however, too greatly fascinated by the tale of the Princess Edain who followed a voice to the land:

"Where nobody gets old and godly and grave,
Where nobody gets old and crafty and wise,
Where nobody gets old and bitter of tongue."

They fall to discussing the fairies, and Mary is warned of the dangers that beset her on Midsummer's Eve. Far from being terrified at the prospect Mary welcomes the thought of release from Bridget's sharp tongue and constant, carping criticism and even invites the fairies to take her. Unwittingly, however, she has placed herself in their power by giving food and drink to some mysterious strangers. Finally she permits a little child whose singing fascinates her to enter the kitchen.

At first the older people believe that the little stranger is the lost child of well-to-do parents and make much of her. Because of her distaste for the crucifix which she terms "ugly," the priest is even persuaded to remove it from the wall and put it out of sight in an inner room.

But presently by various signs the older people realize that the child is not of this world. It is only after Father Hart has removed the crucifix, however, that she is free to work her spell on Mary's soul. With song and dance she utterly fascinates the girl while the peasants gather round Father Hart in abject terror. Too late Mary repents of her willfulness. In the absence of the crucifix the priest is powerless to save her, and the spirit of another mortal is lured away to the "Land of Heart's Desire." Only Mary's lifeless white body is left to the grieving Shawn. She has gone to a land where:

" . . . the fairies dance in a place apart,
Shaking their milk-white feet in a ring,
Tossing their milk-white arms in the air;
For they hear the wind murmur and laugh and sing
Of a land where even the old are fair,
And even the wise are merry of tongue."

John M. Synge

..{ *Born, Rathfarnham, County Dublin, Ireland,* }..
  1871. Died, Dublin, Ireland, 1909

"**B**IOGRAPHICALLY the most remarkable feature of Synge's career was its brevity. In the six years which elapsed between 1903, when *In the Shadow of the Glen* was produced, to 1909, when he died, he rose from absolute obscurity to world fame, and provided us with six plays on which his reputation must rest."[1]

Following the completion, or perhaps we should say, the beginning, of his education at

Trinity College, Dublin, John Millington Synge set out to see the world. On foot he travelled through Germany, Italy and France, absorbing the very essence of them through the lives, legends and literature of their people. It was in 1899 in a Parisian attic that W. B. Yeats discovered him. With the unselfish insight that is not one of the least of Yeats's claims to distinction, he realized that here was real genius being wasted on various kinds of literary hackwork. He persuaded Synge to return to Ireland and devote that genius to the themes of Irish life and the needs of the recently initiated Irish theater movement.

For some time after his return Synge spent his time renewing his kinship with Ireland, sensing the life and belief of its peasantry. Especially was he interested in those islands just off the west coast, and his famous one-act play, *Riders to the Sea*, sums up the essence of the "constant struggle of the islanders against their relentless enemy, the sea."[2] Many critics rate this play as Synge's best in spite of its brevity. Other critics, notably Ernest A. Boyd, in his *Contemporary Drama of Ireland*, pick *The Playboy of the Western World* as Synge's masterpiece. If the number of its productions on the Irish stage be the test of greatness, then this latter play certainly stands first among his limited output. As a matter of fact, it is probably to incidents attending the production of this play that Synge owes the world-wide attention focused on him at the time. Riots attended its appearance not only in Dublin but in our own Philadelphia. Its enemies attacked it as immoral while its proponents quite justly pointed out that it wasn't intended as a "problem" play, and that its morals needed no more defense than did those of Cervantes's famous *Don Quixote*.

The *Well of the Saints* has likewise been made the subject of controversy on the grounds that it is sacrilegious in intent. *In the Shadow of the Glen* faced criticism among the moral patriots as a "hideous slander on Irish womanhood."[3] The posthumous production in 1910 of Synge's unfinished *Deirdre of the Sorrows* emphasized the loss occasioned to the stage by the playwright's early death.

[1,2,3]Ernest A. Boyd in *The Contemporary Drama of Ireland.*

RIDERS TO THE SEA

First produced at Molesworth Hall, Dublin, Feb. 25, 1904.

SCENE: *The kitchen of a peasant's cottage on a small island just off the west coast of Ireland.*

AFTER nine days of constant grieving for her missing son, Michael, who, she feels certain, has been drowned, old Maurya has fallen into a fitful sleep. Her daughter, Cathleen, is busy with household tasks, when another daughter, Nora, slips quietly into the kitchen with a bundle given her by the young priest. It contains part of the clothes taken from the body of a drowned man far in the north. They have been sent to Maurya's cottage with a view to possible identification.

As Maurya shows signs of waking the girls hide the bundle until sometime when they shall be alone. Maurya's grieving for Michael is now coupled with fear of losing Bartley, her only remaining son. Five sons and a husband she has already lost to the sea. Will that insatiable tyrant insist on taking her sixth. The priest says not. But now Bartley insists that he will cross to the mainland this very day, in spite of winds and high seas, to dispose of a horse at the fair.

In a fit of pique at this only remaining son for not listening to her pleas, Maurya lets him go without her blessing. The girls persuade her to intercept him with the lunch they had forgotten to give him and so to make opportunity for that blessing a mother should have given.

While Maurya is gone the girls open the package. The clothes are, indeed, Michael's. Their only comfort is the thought that his body has been given a good Christian burial there in the north where it was washed up. At this point Maurya returns terrified with a vision she had had of Michael riding on the led horse behind Bartley. Now she is sure Bartley is doomed. When the girls show her Michael's clothes her only response is that the good white boards she had bought for his coffin would serve for Bartley instead.

Even as she speaks, the neighboring women troop in, their voices raised in the "keen," that monotonous Irish chant of grief. Men follow bringing the body of Bartley who has been knocked off a cliff into the surf by the horse he was leading. The play closes on the note of Maurya's fatalistic submission. She can sleep now with no worry but that of starvation. "They're all gone now and there isn't anything more the sea can do to me. . . . No man at all can be living forever and we must be satisfied."

Kate

Lord Dunsany

..{ *Born, London, England, 1878* }..

"NEXT to his encouragement of Synge," says the commentator Ernest Boyd,[1] "the incident most to the credit of Yeats' management of the Irish Theater was his immediate recognition of Dunsany's dramatic genius."

Edward John Moreton Drax Plunkett, **Lord Dunsany,** is holder of a title many centuries old and the vast Irish estates that go with it. He was educated at Eton and the English military school at Sandhurst. Following his school days he entered the army and was in active service during the South African troubles at the turn of the century. On his release from the army Dunsany interested himself in the Irish literary movement. His first play, a little one-act dialogue between two burglars who find themselves shut out of Heaven's portal, was produced at the Abbey Theater in 1909 under the title, *The Glittering Gate.* It was followed in 1911 by *King Argimenes and the Unknown Warrior,* produced in Dublin, and *The Gods of the Mountain* which was produced in London in the same year. This latter play and *A Night at an Inn* are generally regarded as Dunsany's two best offerings to date. *If,* produced in London in 1921, enjoyed a long run, possibly because it had a closer connection with real life than any of Dunsany's other plays. *If* was generally regarded as an answer to Barrie's *Dear Brutus.* Barrie supported the theory that a second chance would make no material difference in the outcome of our lives. Dunsany in humorous and effective fashion takes the opposite side of the argument.

Dunsany's plays, on the whole, however, are purely imaginative. Instead of basing them on old Celtic legends he has created legends of his own including a whole new set of oriental dieties. Many of his settings are in fabulous oriental cities and the effect is a rare and delightful combination of oriental mysticism with occidental irony. In the creation of an atmosphere of horror Dunsany often proves himself the equal of Poe.

In answer to a serious-minded lady who inquired of Dunsany as to the significance of some of his plays, the dramatist answered in part:

"I will say first that in my plays I tell very simple stories—so simple that sometimes people of this complex age, being brought up to intricacies, even fail to understand them. . . . I am not trying to teach anybody anything. I merely set out to make a work of art out of a simple theme, and God knows we want works of art in this age of corrugated iron."[2]

If we keep this in mind we will get from Dunsany's plays the unalloyed pleasure the dramatist intended.

[1] In his *The Contemporary Drama of Ireland.*
[2] From Dunsany's *Romance and the Modern Stage,* reprinted in the revised edition of Bierstadt's *Dunsany the Dramatist* and quoted by J. W. Cunliffe in his *Modern English Dramatists.*

A NIGHT AT AN INN

First production in April, 1915, at the Neighborhood Playhouse in Grand Street, New York, with Clayton Hamilton and Alexander Woollcott in the audience.

SCENE: *A room in a deserted inn situated on a lonely moor.*

A PARTY of five desperate English adventurers has stolen a huge ruby which formed the single eye of an oriental jade idol. The idol's three high-priests who pursue the thieves like avenging Furies succeed in destroying two of the conspirators. The surviving trio make their way to England and there enlist the services of "the Toff," a former gentleman ostracized because of his reprehensible habit of winning any card game on which money has been staked.

"The Toff" has rented a deserted inn with the idea of permitting the pursuing priests to catch up with the thieves in a spot where no one is likely to question the priests' disappearance. "The Toff" quite agrees with the estimate of his companions that he "foresees everything." By a clever ruse he tricks the priests into entering the rooms where they are, of course, knifed by his companions. With all three of the idol's avengers lying dead in the room, it seems to the three sailors a fitting time to toast the mastermind that has freed them from pursuit. The corpses, they decide, can wait a bit for their burial in the cellar.

The group begins to drink and to plan for disposal of the ruby in London. In the midst of their celebration stony footfalls are heard without and a sense of impending doom takes possession of the group. The door opens and the huge jade idol gropes his way to the table, feels for the ruby and screws it into the socket in his forehead. His sight restored the idol strides firmly from the room.

The thieves forget to mourn the loss of the jewel in their relief at being freed from that awful presence. Just as their feelings are returning to normal a voice is heard from without calling the name of one of the sailors. Try as he will, the victim cannot escape the compulsion of that voice. He leaves by the door through which the idol had departed and a moan is heard from without. One of the party, looking from the window, verifies the awful cause of that single moan but neither he nor his companion can resist the voice when in turn it pronounces their names.

"The Toff" has looked on unmoved. His hitherto fertile brain has apparently no suggestion to offer to the despairing appeals of his fellow-conspirators. But when finally the voice speaks his name, he finds himself, too, powerless to disobey. He goes out remarking: "I did not forsee it."

Sean O'Casey

..{ *Born, Dublin, Ireland, 1884* }..

NO DISCUSSION of Irish drama is complete without Sean O'Casey's almost photographically real pictures of Irish tenement life. Professor J. W. Cunliffe of Columbia University goes so far as to say that O'Casey is "the greatest discovery since the War, not only of the Abbey Theater but of European drama."[1]

Sean O'Casey is himself a product of the Dublin tenements. His father died when he was three and his mother managed some way to keep her little brood together. Their morning meal was dry bread and tea and, if they were lucky, they had dry bread and tea again for supper. When O'Casey was fourteen he taught himself to read. From then on, any money that could possibly be spared from the bare necessities, went into books. As for formal education, he had none.

Perhaps this very lack was a blessing in disguise. Knowing no rules for the building of successful drama except such as he had observed from his own reading, especially of Shakspere, he was free to build his dramas of Irish tenement life as he saw it. If, breaking all accepted rules, tragedy and comedy follow on each other's heels, it is because they have done so in the playwright's own life. All his plays are tragic in intent but three-fourths of the dialogue stirs the audience to laughter.

O'Casey knows the bitter enmities of the Irish struggle for self-expression first hand, for he was a part of the Citizen Army. He has seen neighbor kill neighbor in the mad frenzy of religious clashes and has later seen bitter enemies weeping together over the coffins of their victims. Those unforgettable pictures photographed in his brain he has reproduced in his plays.

The playwright's first accepted play, *The Shadow of a Gunman*, was produced April 12, 1923, at the Abbey Theater, Dublin. When his second play, *Juno and the Paycock*, entered a successful run in London, he felt free to leave his job as a bricksetter's helper and give his full attention to writing. His third play, *The Plough and the Stars*, created almost as much of a riot at its first production in the Abbey Theater as had Synge's *Playboy of the Western World*, and led Yeats to exclaim to the unruly audience: "You have again rocked the cradle of genius."

O'Casey's most recent play to appear in America is *Within the Gates*. It was recently forbidden the stage in Boston, thus adding not a little to its interest for playgoers in other cities.

[1] In his *Modern English Playwrights*.

JUNO AND THE PAYCOCK

Produced at the Abbey Theater, Dublin, March 3, 1924; at the Mayfair Theater, New York, March 15, 1926.

SCENE: *The combination kitchen-living-bedroom of the Boyle's two-room flat.*

CAPTAIN BOYLE is "Captain" by virtue of a single trip made as seaman on a collier bound from London to Liverpool. He is usually known to his neighbors, however, as the "paycock" on account of his strutting, consequential gait. He is a worthless toper and idler, but withal, possesses a certain rough eloquence of expression. He and his crony, Joxer, spend most of their time drinking in "pubs" or playing cards in the Boyle flat, where Joxer flatters him to his face and steals from him behind his back. Boyle has nicknamed his wife "Juno" because she "was born and christened in June. I met her in June; we were married in June an' Johnny was born in June."

The son, Johnny, is a cripple and practically a nervous wreck due to a bullet received in the Easter Week Rebellion of 1916. His nervousness and irritability increase almost to mania when he learns through a newspaper that one of his former "Die-hard" comrades, Bobbie Tancred, has been killed because of information that Johnny has given the authorities.

The daughter, Mary, through reading has acquired a taste for better things, and longs for a different sort of life. She has discarded one suitor, Jerry Devine, a trades-union organizer, in favor of slick young Charles Bentham, a school teacher and law student. This, she feels, may be a step toward realizing her ambitions. Bentham tells the family that they are about to inherit a legacy from a relative. There can be no doubt about it, because he himself has drawn the will.

On the strength of their expectations, the Boyle family goes on a spending spree. They borrow from their neighbors and stretch their credit with the local tradesmen to the utter-most limit. Two months later both the Boyles and their creditors learn that the legacy is uncollectible due to Bentham's clumsiness in drafting the will. Thenceforward Bentham loses his interest in Mary, although she is shortly to bear his child. As if all this were not tragedy enough, the Irregular Mobilizers learn of Johnny's part in Bobbie Tancred's death and hurry him off to his doom for betrayal of a comrade. An hour later Mrs. Boyle is summoned by the police to identify her son's body.

Through it all the Paycock and his friend, Joxer, remain gloriously drunk, and it is the Paycock who speaks the final words of the play: "The whole world's in a terrible state of chaos."

Luigi Pirandello

..{ *Born, Girgenti, Sicily, 1867* }..

TOWARD the close of 1934, when the Swedish Academy of Literature in Stockholm looked around to see what man in the field of literature had produced the most distinguished work of an idealistic tendency, their choice fell on Luigi Pirandello, an Italian novelist and playwright, native of Sicily.

Luigi Pirandello spent the first nineteen years of his life uneventfully in Sicily. When he was nineteen he went to Rome to study at the university, and in 1891 went to Germany where he presently received a degree in Philosophy and philology from the University of Bonn. Until comparatively recently (1923) he has taught in Rome in the Women's Higher Normal School.

Pirandello wrote novels and short stories during some thirty years before he began writing for the stage. For the most part they created no great stir even in his native Italy. Some critics claim that the reason for the lack of interest in Pirandello's writings is inherent in the stories themselves; others, that the lack of recognition was due to the fact that he was a genius a quarter-century ahead of his time.

Probably the best known of his novels is *The Late Mattia Pascal* which appeared in 1904. It is the story of a man who shams death, then tries in vain to begin life anew in a different atmosphere and under another name. Pirandello's short stories have been gathered together in one volume under the title, *Novelle per un Anno* . . . a collected edition of 365 short stories, one for every day in the year.

With his dramatic work Pirandello sprang suddenly into the fame that was denied his strictly literary efforts. So far as the writer can ascertain his first produced play was *Sicilian Limes*. The play that brought him prominence, however, both in Italy and in foreign countries, was *Six Characters in Search of an Author*. In this play he introduces the design with which all his subsequent plays deal to a greater or lesser extent . . . the ambiguous relationship between reality and belief. *Six Characters*, however, is more than the expounding of a theory; it is likewise more than just a "trick" play. It is a dramatization of the artistic process of creation, whether for the stage or the novel.

Other plays well known to the literati if not to the general public are: *Right You Are*, *Henry IV*, and *As You Desire Me*. Since the awarding of the Nobel prize Pirandello's *Tonight We Improvise* has been staged in Paris. The only comment of the critics was a non-committal "interesting."

SIX CHARACTERS IN SEARCH OF AN AUTHOR

First New York production at the Princess Theater, October 30, 1922.

SCENE: *The stage of an empty theater set for rehearsal.*

A STOCK company under the direction of their Manager and with the assistance of the Prompter and the Property Man is about to rehearse a play. Since there is a dearth of good French comedies, they have to fall back on a comedy by Pirandello, which, the Manager admits, is, as usual, quite incomprehensible. Just as rehearsal starts the Door Man interrupts. He is followed by a queer assortment of Characters who announce that they are looking for an author.

It appears that the author whose imagination has conceived them has decided against putting them in a drama. Their only chance to live is to find some author who is willing to put them in a play. The bewildered Manager finally consents to let the Characters live out their own story on the stage, while the Prompter takes down the parts in shorthand and the stock company stands round to pick up suggestions for proper interpretation. The action proceeds accompanied by the attempts of the harassed Manager to keep it within the selective and arbitrary requirements of the stage, and by the insistent endeavors of the Characters to act out the whole of their internal struggle

The Machiavellian brain of the Father has conceived the idea of sending his wife away with his secretary, since the two are obviously mentally and spiritually mated. He thinks to watch the experiment from a bystander's position. However, he soon loses sight of the artificially created Family who, after the death of the Man, are in dire poverty. The comely elder daughter falls into the hands of a modern Procuress, and the Father renews his contact with the Family through an assignation with this girl. When he learns their circumstances, the Father insists that the Mother and her three illegitimate children come home with him.

The legitimate Son, grown to manhood, scorns them all. The Mother, on the contrary, has eyes only for her legitimate Son, and, driven by his coldness, attempts suicide in the garden fountain.

When the Son runs to rescue her, he sees the body of the little four-year-old Sister in the fountain while the fourteen-year-old Brother stands by staring at it with a look of madness in his eyes. Then before anyone can interfere the Boy has slipped behind a tree and shot himself.

The Manager is inclined to think that this will make a fine climax to an impressive play until he discovers that it was not pretense but reality. In disgust he exclaims: "To Hell with it! I've lost a whole day over these people, a whole day!"

W. Somerset Maugham

..{ *Born, Paris, France, 1874* }..

EVERYONE who pretends to any knowledge of contemporary theater knows Somerset Maugham's "brilliantly witty but shamelessly cynical"[1] satire for the stage, *Our Betters*. To paraphrase, *Our Betters* was just what the public ordered, but it took an accident to discover originally that Maugham could give the public what they apparently wanted just a little better than anyone else. A London producer, hunting for something with which to keep his theater open just a little later in the spring, came upon a stack of dusty manuscripts awaiting return to their authors in a fellow producer's office. Glancing them over he decided that Maugham's *Lady Frederick* would "get by," and in no time found himself with the hit of the season. Almost at once other producers dug up rejected plays by the same author, and presently four of Maugham's plays were running concurrently and playing to capacity houses. One critic even remarked that it would probably be safe to fill every theater in London with Maugham's discarded plays.

Somerset Maugham, an Englishman born in Paris, was educated at King's College, Canterbury, and the University of Heidelberg, and served an interneship at St. Thomas's Hospital. During the war he served both in his professional capacity as a physician and also in the secret service. In this latter capacity he acquired the first-hand knowledge on which he based the plot and settings of his famous novel, *Ashenden*. While in Russia during the war he developed tuberculosis, and *Moon and Sixpence*, one of the most famous of his later novels, was written upon a hospital cot. It was his short story, *Miss Thompson*, appearing in *Smart Set* which served as the basis for John Colton's and Clemence Randolph's successful melodrama, *Rain*, starring Jeanne Eagels, and recently revived by Tallulah Bankhead.

So far as American audiences are concerned the better known of Maugham's plays are: *Cæsar's Wife*, *East of Suez*, *The Constant Wife* (played most effectively by Ethel Barrymore), *The Circle*, rated by some critics as his best, and *The Letter*. Maugham himself prefers *The Land of Promise*, a play little known in America.

Maugham, the man, is shy, reserved, and stutters most embarrassingly. He finds it hard to talk to strangers and almost never gives interviews. His famous novel, *Of Human Bondage*, is supposed to be a faithful record of the first thirty years of his own life. Recently a mother wrote to Maugham for advice as to how to start her son in a literary career. Maugham's brief reply was: "Give him $1000 a year for five years and tell him to go to the devil."

[1]*Encyclopedia Britannica*, 14th edition.

OUR BETTERS

Produced by John D. Williams at the Hudson Theater, New York, March 12, 1917, with Chrystal Herne taking the part of Lady Grayston.

SCENE: *The action takes place first at Lady Graystone's house in Grosvenor Street, Mayfair, on a fine spring day, and four weeks later at Feathers Nevil, her husband's country place in Suffolk.*

BESSIE SAUNDERS, a pretty American girl with a million dollar fortune, is the guest of her sister, Lady Grayston. The latter, through lavish expenditures, a flair for publicity, and an invincible determination, has succeeded in forcing her way into London society. Her parties are attended by all . . . well, by nearly all . . . the "elite."

Lady Grayston is now intent on securing a title for Bessie. So far she has exploited her sister so successfully that Lord Harry Bleane, an ordinary but wholesome young Englishman, is on the point of proposing. In fact, Bessie is unable to stall him off any longer, and before the end of Act I she has promised that she will give him his answer four weeks hence at the house party at Feathers Nevil.

The house party in question is made up of Lady Grayston's constant companions: Clay Thornton, an American who has succeeded in making himself a London man-about-town, and has the reputation of sacrificing his best friends for the sake of an amusing story; the wealthy Duchesse de Surenne, an American divorcée, who is infatuated with her latest gigolo, Tony Paxton; the Princess della Circola, another rich American separated from her titled husband; Arthur Fenwick, a pompous elderly American, who pays part of the expense of Lady Grayston's magnificent entertainments, and plays host in her husband's absence; and, of course, Lord Harry Bleane. George, Lady Grayston's husband, is, as usual, noticeably absent from his wife's party.

Of late Tony has been casting amorous eyes on his hostess, and the Duchesse is worried about retaining her hold over him. Surrendering to a momentary fascination, Lady Grayston keeps a rendezvous with Tony, against her better judgment, and the Duchesse in a hysterical scene before the entire house party accuses the pair. What concerns Lady Grayston most is how to prevent her house party from breaking up, and thus making herself the laughing stock of London society. It is of equal importance that she placate Fenwick, for if she should lose his financial support, her present mode of living would be frankly impossible. With her usual aplomb and executive ability she accomplishes both difficult ends.

Bessie has been on the point of accepting Lord Harry. Now she realizes that she could never fit into the dull English society of which Harry's wife should be a part, nor does she wish to accept the alternative of her sister's crowd. She compromises by taking the next boat back to America along with her young American admirer, Fleming Harvey.

John Galsworthy

..{ *Born, Coombe, Surrey, England, 1867* }..
{ *Died, Hampstead, England, 1933* }

THE novelist and playwright, John Galsworthy, seems to have been born under a
lucky star. Not only did he make his entrance
into the world under the sponsorship of a
family of culture, well able to give him an
excellent education; but the moment he chose
for his entry into the world of drama was when
the pioneer work for his particular type had
already been done by Jones and Pinero, Shaw
and Barrie. Theater audiences were ready for
John Galsworthy.

The playwright was the son of a leading
London lawyer. His formal education was
acquired at Harrow and Oxford and finished off
with a year's travel. He had studied law but
preferred novel writing, and it was to this that
he gave his immediate attention. It was not
until 1906 that his first drama, *The Silver Box*,
was produced at the Royal Court Theater,
London. From that time up to the World War,
Galsworthy was a more or less steady contribu-
tor to the stage. Secure in the possession of
private means, and already receiving considerable in royalties from his novels, he was under
no economic compulsion in his dramatic writing.
He was at the outset, and remained in all his
plays, a conscientious artist.

With the outbreak of the war, Galsworthy
interrupted his writing career to serve most
inconspicuously as a masseur in a French
hospital. He returned to the stage in 1920 with
The Skin Game, a phrase he had picked up on a
recent trip to America. That play and many
others from his pen have enjoyed enthusiastic
American reception, among them: *The Mob,
Strife, The Pigeon, Justice, The Eldest Son, Old
English, Escape*, and *Loyalties*. The latter play
expresses Galsworthy's view that loyalty to
one's race or nation or club, commendable as
it may be, is not a sufficient guide for the
complex situations of life.

In his plays Galsworthy has pictured from a
first hand acquaintance the upper half of English
society. His plays show no villains and few
heroes. He simply pictures social conditions as
they are. He realizes the inadequacy of modern
social and industrial organization but believes
that oppressor as well as oppressed is the victim
of forces beyond the power of the individual
to alter.

Galsworthy may not have had the zeal of a
Shaw for reform; but, according to Professor J.
W. Cunliffe of Columbia, he had more balance
and greater artistic power. His rule of dramatic
writing throughout was: "Take care of
character; action and dialogue will take care
of themselves."[1] In the field of novel writing,
probably his best known work is the sequence
generally known as the *Forsyte Saga*.

[1] Cunliffe in his *Modern English Playwrights.*

LOYALTIES

First American production September 27, 1922, by Charles Dillingham at the Gaiety Theater, New York, following a sensational London run.

SCENE: *The country house of the Charles Winsors; a London club; a solicitor's office; the flat of the Dancys.*

FERDINAND DE LEVIS, a young Jew with social aspirations, is a member of the house party being entertained by Charles and Lady Adela Winsor. The party has just separated for the night, when De Levis comes to the Winsors' rooms to announce that he has been robbed of nearly one thousand pounds. He insists that the police be called.

The officers of the law, however, can only point out that the thief must have entered by the open window. After their departure, De Levis confides to General Conynge, a fellow guest, that he knows the thief and names Captain Dancy, also a guest. Just before dinner Dancy has made a standing jump onto a narrow four-foot bookcase. De Levis assumes that he could easily jump the seven feet that separates the two balconies. Besides, Dancy is known to be pressed for cash.

General Conynge is outraged at this accusation against an English gentleman and officer. Privately, however, he is upset, because during the investigation he has noticed that Dancy's coat sleeve was wet as though from rain, Dancy, of course, claims to have been in the hall writing letters. Under threat of social ostracism, De Levis is persuaded to drop the matter. At length, however, in a club to which both men belong, he voices his suspicions.

Although Dancy is noticeably reluctant to do so, his friends insist that he bring civil action against De Levis. In an effort to avoid the courts, Dancy tries to force De Levis into a duel with the supreme insult "damned Jew." From that point on De Levis is deaf to all pleas for mercy. He is fighting for the honor of his race, as his antagonists are fighting for the "honor of an English gentleman."

As the trial progresses one of the stolen bank-notes is brought to the office of Dancy's solicitor, and Dancy is revealed as the man who passed it. His solicitors promptly withdraw from the case which is tantamount to confessing their client's guilt. Although De Levis is satisfied to let the matter drop with his vindication, the Law steps in to arrest Dancy.

The latter confesses to his bride that he stole the money to settle a debt of honor with a woman of his bachelor days. His wife offers to flee with him, but rather than drag her down into an ignominy from which there is no recovery, he shoots himself just as the arresting officers enter the flat.

St. John Ervine

..{ *Born, Belfast, Ireland, 1883* }..

THERE seems to be a wide divergence of opinion among critics as to whether St. John Ervine has or has not a dramatic message for the world. As to the soundness of his work as a theatrical critic and as to the value of his critical essays, commentators are agreed. Perhaps his rating as a dramatist is determined somewhat by the depth and character of the commentator's interest in the Irish National Theater movement.

Ervine, though an Ulsterman by birth, is not usually considered an integral part of the Irish Theater movement, in spite of the fact that he was for a time director of the Abbey Theater. He had preferred to seek the acclaim of the wider public offered for his undoubted journalistic talents in the far larger and more important London. It was only when the fame of the Irish Theater movement had spread beyond the borders of Ireland and Irish plays had become popular in London that he associated himself with the movement. It was at that time (1911) that Ervine's first produced play, *Mixed Marriage*, was presented in the Abbey Theater and became an immediate success. There are those who claim that Ervine's only interest in the Irish Theater is personal and pecuniary. Perhaps it is simply another case of a "prophet in his own country."

His first drama, *Mixed Marriage*, is powerfully motivated. The characters are drawn with a fine knowledge of the life of the Belfast industrial classes and of the religious bigotry that prevents their uniting in their own interests. A later play, *John Ferguson*, centered around the tribulations of an Irish peasant of that name, was presented in America with remarkable success by the Theater Guild during the season of 1918-1919. *Jane Clegg*, produced in England prior to the production of *John Ferguson*, is a sordid drama of English lower-middle-class life, photographically realistic in detail.

It is doubtful, however, whether drama is Ervine's best medium of expression. As one critic puts it, his characters are too prone to become mere "verbal statements of a point of view."[1] They lack the breath of life—a soul of their own. Some critics claim that two of his novels, *Mrs. Martin's Man* and *Changing Winds*, are much better than his dramas. Despite all the critics say, one thing is certain. However you rate St. John Ervine, no study of present-day drama is complete without at least a glance at his work.

[1] Ernest A. Boyd in *The Contemporary Drama of Ireland.*

JANE CLEGG

First presented in Miss Horniman's Theater, Manchester, in 1913 and later in London. Produced in New York by the Theater Guild, February 23, 1920.

SCENE: *The living room of the Clegg home in a small English town.*

HENRY CLEGG'S family is awaiting his late homecoming. From the conversation between his wife, Jane, and Grandma Clegg we learn that Henry is none too stable where women are concerned; also, that Jane has refused to give him a recently inherited legacy so that he may set himself up in business.

When Henry finally arrives his excuses are thin and he seems glad to change the subject. A letter has arrived containing a check made out in his name for a sum owed his firm.

"Now if I wasn't honest . . . !" exclaims Henry.

As they talk a Mr. Munce arrives to see Henry "on business," and the women go off to bed. Mr Munce turns out to be a bookie to whom Henry owes money. He threatens, unless he is paid, to tell Jane about a woman he has seen Henry with. Henry, thinking to appeal to Munce's sympathy, confesses that the girl is going to have a child. If he could only lay hands on the money, he'd take her off to Canada.

Two evenings later, when the family are again awaiting for Henry, Mr. Morrison, the bookkeeper from the firm's office, arrives. Henry has not been at the office all day and the money from the check he had received has not been turned in. At this point Henry enters, and when Jane realizes that he has actually taken the money, she agrees to make it good. Henry's excuse is that the firm made him stand the bad debts in his territory and so he got into debt himself. When Mr. Morrison returns the following day for the money, however, Jane learns that this is a lie. She refuses to pay out the money until she learns what Henry has done with the cash from the check. Finally he claims to have paid a gambling debt to Munce, but this story, too, is proven false when Munce arrives in a rage because he hasn't been paid.

Then the whole story of Henry's duplicity comes out, even to the fact that he had used the money to buy tickets for Canada. He tells Jane that he has been false to her because she was hard and unsympathetic, and because he couldn't stand preaching nor living with someone who was better than himself. With Kitty he is happy because Kitty is weak like himself. So in the end Jane sends him off to Canada with his "fancy woman," and takes upon herself the responsibility of Grandma Clegg and the children.

Mrs. Clegg, the doting grandmother

Ferenc Molnar

..{ *Born, Budapest, Hungary, 1878* }..

MODERN Hungarian drama is known to America largely through the plays of Ferenc Molnar, not only because he is one of the leading Hungarian dramatists, but because so few Hungarian playwrights have received

English translation. The critic, Robert Garland, rates Molnar's *Liliom* as one of the finest of modern plays. If, however, one tries to "understand" *Liliom*, it will probably lose half its charm. It should be enjoyed for what it is, a fantastic, poetic play, as are the other six or seven of Molnar's which have been translated.

Ferenc Molnar (better known, perhaps, as Franz) is the son of wealthy Jewish parents. He graduated from the Universities of Geneva and Budapest. His literary career, however, began even earlier when, at the age of eighteen, he wrote "short sketches and humorous dialogues of such beauty and charm that he became a national figure almost at once, and the circulation of his newspaper increased until it was the foremost in Budapest,"[1] according to the commentator, Barrett H. Clark. Presently he married Margaret Vaszi, the daughter of his editor, herself a well-known journalist. This marriage ended in divorce after two years, and later he married the Hungarian actress, Sari Fedak, who had enacted rôles in his own plays. This marriage, also, turned out unfortunately.

While Molnar is known outside Hungary almost exclusively as a dramatist, in his native land he ranks high as a novelist, short story writer, and a journalist of ability. During the World War he served at the front as war correspondent.

An interesting difference between the American stage and the foreign stage is brought to light by the New York production of *Liliom*. In the American production a handsome and attractive actor played the title rôle and a beautiful and sophisticated actress took the part of Julie. On the German stage (Berlin, 1923) Max Pallenberg, a gifted but exceedingly homely actor, played the part of the "roughneck," Liliom, and the exceptional Lucie Hoflich, who weighs some two hundred pounds gave a much more believable portrayal of the ignorant servant girl. American audiences apparently like even their art sugar-coated.

Other Molnar plays known in America either through translation or adaptation are *The Swan, The Guardsman, Fashions for Men,* and *The Play's the Thing.*

[1] In *A Study of the Modern Drama.*

LILIOM

First produced in Budapest in December,1909,but withdrawn after thirty-odd performances. Revived after the World War, it enjoyed a great continental success and was produced in America by the Theater Guild, April 20, 1921, at the Garrick Theater with Eva Le Galli- enne as Julie and Joseph Schildkraut as Liliom.

SCENE: *The grounds of an amusement park and vicinity.*

LILIOM (in free translation a "tough") is a barker in Madame Muskat's amusement park. He is valuable because he attracts feminine trade. The proprietress, however, is herself in love with Liliom, and when she sees Julie and Marie flirting with him she orders them out of the park. This outrages Liliom's spirit of independence. He takes up Julie's defense and is fired.

In spite of the warnings of two policemen Julie remains with Liliom in the park. Liliom's interest in Julie is piqued by the girl's simplicity and her absolute lack of fear of him. They even tentatively discuss marriage. Apparently, however, it is without benefit of clergy that we find them a little later living in the "dilapi- dated hovel" where Mother Hollunder, Julie's aunt, has her photograph studio.

Because Julie is reasonable and right in all their arguments and because he cannot stand it to see her cry, Liliom beats her. Her aunt and Marie want her to leave Liliom and marry the widower carpenter. Julie refuses, and when Madame Muskat comes to induce Liliom to return to his job with her, Julie insists that she has something to tell Liliom privately that can't wait.

The news that he is to become a father stirs Liliom's interest in acquiring money. Curtly dismissing Madame Muskat he plots with the "Sparrow" the details of a holdup they have been tentatively discussing. Their plans go awry and Liliom prefers suicide to jail. Before he dies, however, he tries to explain to Julie that he beat her because he couldn't stand it to be always in the wrong. He advises her to marry the carpenter, but she refuses.

In the court of Heaven Liliom is sentenced to sixteen years in the purifying flames, after which he is to have one day on earth. The good deed that he shall do on that day for his daughter yet to be born will determine his permanent place in Heaven. When Liliom's day on earth finally comes, unrecognized by Julie, he offers his daughter, Louise, a star stolen from the firmament. Julie scorns his gift with the remark that it is probably stolen, and at this he slaps Louise's hand as hard as he can. Louise cannot understand why it felt only like a caress, but her mother explains that it is possible for someone to "beat you and beat you and beat you and still not hurt you at all."

Eugene O'Neill

..{ *Born, New York City, 1888* }..

EUGENE GLADSTONE O'NEILL, rated the foremost American dramatist, piled a lifetime of adventurous living into his first twenty-seven years. He covered (under protest) the theatrical barrens of "the road" with his father's stock company. Later Wanderlust took him from New York to Buenos Aires, from South America to South Africa and back again to South America because he couldn't convince the South African authorities that he had a

visible means of support. He held jobs that varied from secretary of a mail order house to gold prospecting in Central America; from draughtsman for Westinghouse Electric Co. to mule tender on tramp steamers; from beach comber to newspaper reporter. It was in this latter job, when he was 27, that Fate in the form of certain lung spots caught up with him and he was sentenced to a year in a sanitorium.

This year was for O'Neill a spiritual as well as a physical rebirth. He returned to life with a sure knowledge of what he wanted to do and a varied background of experience upon which to call in doing it. Leaving the sanitorium, O'Neill turned to Professor George Pierce Baker's "English 47" at Harvard for a serious study of dramatic technique. His first contacts with the stage as a playwright were in the "Little Theater" movement in Province-town. There his first produced play, *Bound East for Cardiff*, was enacted. His first full length play, *Beyond the Horizon*, not only achieved production on commercially-minded Broadway, but incidentally won the Pulitzer Prize for that year.

O'Neill's first real box office success, however, was *Anna Christie*. It was probably the furore of discussion aroused by the novelty both of theme and treatment in *Strange Interlude* (1928) that made O'Neill's name known wherever the English-speaking stage is discussed. Critics disagree as to which of his plays is actually best. The writer agrees with Robert Garland, dramatic critic of the *New York World-Telegram*, in his unhesitating choice of *Beyond the Horizon*. According to the commentator, Burns Mantle, this play is the tragedy of a dreamer who lacked the courage to live his dream. To me it is rather the tragedy of a man caught in the snare of an unsuitable young love; bound by the circumstances of an unfortunate marriage within narrow and appressive horizons from which death alone can free him.

Other much discussed plays of this dramatist include *The Emperor Jones, Mourning Becomes Electra,* and *All God's Chillun Got Wings.*

BEYOND THE HORIZON

First production by John D. Williams at a special matinée performance at the Morosco Theater, New York City, February 2, 1920.

SCENE: *The fields and farmhouse of the New England home of the Mayo family.*

THE two sons of the Mayo family, although totally unlike, are bound together by a strong brotherly affection. To Robert, the frail youth fond of books and dreaming, "the far places of the world beckon alluringly." Andrew finds the flowering of all his hopes in the homely tasks of the farm. Both young men love Ruth Atkins, the pretty daughter of a neighboring widow. At the opening of the play Robert is on the eve of departure for a world voyage on his uncle's ship. Only one regret mars his anticipation . . . that he might not have had Ruth's affection. Then unexpectedly he learns that he is the girl's choice, and promptly, albeit somewhat regretfully, gives up his plans for sailing.

Andrew enters the room as Robert is telling his parents and uncle of his changed intentions. The older brother promptly announces the resolve to sail in Robert's place. The subsequent death of his father throws on Robert a responsibility for which he is totally unfitted, and the family gradually sinks into deep poverty.

In a fit of anger and thwarted ambition, Ruth confesses one day to Robert that four months after her marriage she knew her mistake; that Andrew was the one she really loves. Shortly thereafter the prosperous Andrew returns on a visit and, lest the shadow of Ruth should lie between them, tells his brother that he has entirely recovered from any affection he had earlier imagined for Ruth. When he repeats this conversation to Ruth, he cannot understand her hysterical reaction: "You told him that? You actually told him that?"

With the death of their sickly child, Mary, Robert loses his last interest in life. His own death from the tuberculosis that has so long threatened is very near. Ruth pockets her pride and wires Andrew, but it is too late. Andrew arrives just before Robert's death, and Ruth confesses that long ago she had told Robert that she loved Andrew. Andrew, with his affection for his dying brother uppermost in his consciousness, is horrified. He exacts from the girl the promise that she will tell Robert before he dies that she had really loved him all the time. When she enters the bedroom she finds that Robert has already passed "beyond the horizon" to the fulfillment of his longings. All Andrew can say as he shakes Ruth roughly is: "He's gone and you never told him! You never told him!"

Maxwell Anderson *and* Laurence Stallings

..{ *Maxwell Anderson, born, Atlantic, Pennsylvania, 1888*
Laurence Stallings, born, Macon, Georgia, 1894 }..

BOTH Maxwell Anderson and Laurence Stallings are among the great throng of writers and dramatists who have been graduated from a newspaper office . . . in their particular case, Mr. Pulitzer's *New York Morning World*. Probably the most important claim either of them can make to dramatic fame rests at present on that striking result of their collaboration, *What Price Glory*.

This play, a vital recapitulation of war and post-war days by men who knew those days at first hand, was the forerunner of a whole series of plays whose characters spoke the language of the life they were portraying. But the play's overnight success was due no more to the fact that a post-war generation was ready for just such a searching mirror of war and war problems than it was tribute to the fact that out of their own personal experiences and sufferings these men had made a vital and actable drama.

Mr. Anderson is the son of a Baptist minister, which accounts for his first-hand acquaintance with a large number of sovereign states. Perhaps it also accounts for the fact that his first years out of college were spent in the teaching profession in North Dakota, at Leland Stanford University and at Whittier College, California. Needing more money than teaching afforded, he optimistically turned to newspaper work, writing editorials for the *San Francisco Bulletin*. Presently he was fired for being too outspoken, and at length reached the *Morning World* and Broadway. Mr Anderson has to his personal credit, among others, the plays: *Saturday's Children, Gypsy, Both Your Houses, Elizabeth the Queen*, and *Valley Forge*.

Laurence Stallings, as a reporter on the *Atlanta Journal*, was assigned to write up the story of how army recruiting was being carried on in his native state. During his first-hand investigation he apparently sold himself on the desirability of becoming a Marine forthwith. He wrote the story he had been sent to get, resigned his job and subsequently landed in France with the Fifth Marines. Wounded at Belleau Wood, he spent most of the next three years in hospitals, escaping only by the costly expedient of leaving a leg behind.

Thereafter he took a master's degree at Georgetown University in our national capital and taught for a while in that institution. Presently he returned to newspaper work via Mr. Hearst's *Washington Times*, thence to the *New York World* and *What Price Glory*.

Mr. Stallings is the author of the war novel, *Plumes*. His wife, the former Helen Purefoy Poteat, is the "unknown soldier" of his magazine stories.

WHAT PRICE GLORY

Produced September 5, 1924, in New York and played for 299 performances.

SCENE: *At the front in the zone of advance, 1918.*

THE opening action of *What Price Glory* takes place at company headquarters of an outfit of marines in a French village. Corporals Gowdy, Kiper, and Lipinsky are discussing wars and women, particularly the latter. Talk turns to the amours of their commanding officer, Captain Flagg, who has appropriated for himself the only attractive girl in the village, Charmaine, daughter of Cognac Pete. Since Captain Flagg is a "hard customer" when sober and worse still when drunk, there seems to be nothing they can do about it.

Into this conversation comes Sergeant Quirt, a practical soldier and a "devil with the women." He has served with Captain Flagg before in various corners of the world. Both men have an enormous respect for each other's soldiering abilities, but they are constantly at loggerheads over affairs of the heart. Captain Flagg departs on a ten-day leave, warning Charmaine to stay away from soldiers while he is gone, especially the new top sergeant.

Flagg is hardly out of sight, however, before she is making up to the not unwilling Sergeant Quirt. Thus Captain Flagg returns to a pretty mess. Cognac Pete comes to complain of the rape of his daughter by an American soldier which is a hanging matter, or, if you prefer, a marrying matter. This, from the Captain's viewpoint, of course, is just as bad. When, however, Pete names Sergeant Quirt instead of himself, he is gleeful at the chance to pay off former defeats by marrying Quirt to the girl and making him sign over his soldier pay.

Orders for the company's immediate advance put a stop to these plans. Even for the sake of a sweet revenge, Captain Flagg will not spoil a good top sergeant by marriage when there's soldiering to be done. Under fire in German territory both Flagg and Quirt are brave, tireless, understanding and sympathetic. The irrepressible Quirt is wounded and sent to the hospital. When he hears, however, that his company has earned a month's leave by capturing a "German officer of Alsatian birth," he escapes in his pajamas to beat Flagg back to company headquarters and Charmaine. When Flagg arrives they stake Charmaine's kisses on the turn of a card. Flagg gets no chance to enjoy the fruits of victory for the company's leave is suddenly cancelled, and they are ordered back to the front. Hastily kissing Charmaine, Quirt limps after the others, calling, "Papa Flagg, wait for your top sergeant!"

Marc Connelly

..{*Born, McKeesport, Pennsylvania, 1891*}..

LIKE uncountable others of his fellow playwrights, Marc Connelly reached the stage
via the newspaper route. Perhaps if the ancient
Greeks had had daily news sheets Aristophanes
might have started his career as a Grecian
Westbrook Pegler, and it is still more certain
that Aristotle would have held down the post
of dramatic critic.

Mr. Connelly's claim to fame, we believe,
rests on *Green Pastures*, that epic of colored
religion suggested to the author by the Old
Testament stories of Roark Bradford in his
Ol' Man Adam an' His Chillun. This play, to

quote Burns Mantle, is "a naive retelling of
the Old Testament as a colored preacher in
Louisiana might tell it to his Sunday School
class."[1] Another critic has called it the "divine
comedy of the modern theater."[2] Following
640 consecutive performances on Broadway
Green Pastures went on the road and as this
book goes to press has some five years later
just finished a second successful New York run
and a total of well over 1700 performances.
During these five years it has netted its authors
royalties amounting to $296,563 up to the end
of week before it closed (*New York Times*
figures) which should make up for any lingering
disappointment Mr. Connelly might feel over
that first flop.

It is almost as difficult to get information
about the lives of our present playwrights as
about an Aristophanes or a Thomas Kyd. All
in all they're an exceptionally modest and
retiring lot. But whatever his private life
may be we venture the prophecy that Marc
Connelly will live for future generations in his
modern Morality, *Green Pastures*.

Mr. Connelly, however, went no farther
afield than Pittsburgh where, after some higher
Education at Trinity Hall, in Washington,
Pennsylvania, he began his business and literary
career on a Pittsburgh daily. In the course of
events he wrote and sold some lyrics for a
musical comedy destined for New York production. When the opening night came he
optimistically boarded a train and came to the
metropolis to share the glory. The play was
a complete flop. Not prepared for such an
eventuality, Connelly did not have the return
fare to Pittsburgh and possibly said to himself:
"Who wants to live in Pittsburgh, anyway?"

At any rate, from that time on New York
supported him although not very generously
until after the beginning of the notable collaboration with George S. Kaufmann. The
results of this partnership include among others:
Dulcy, *To the Ladies*, *Helen of Troy, N. Y.*, and
Beggars on Horseback. Mr Connelly, however,
was gradually finding in himself a predilection
for the more serious drama, so that it seemed
best for these two collaborators to go their
separate ways.

[1] In his *Best Plays of 1929-30*.
[2] Quoted by Mantle in his *Best Plays of 1929-30* without original source.

GREEN PASTURES

Produced February 26, 1930, at the Mansfield Theater by Laurence Rivers, Inc. (Rowland Stebbins) and as this is written has passed its 1675th performance The play was awarded the Pulitzer Prize for 1930.

SCENE: *A Biblical Heaven and earth such as might be conceived in the minds of illiterate southern negroes.*

MR. DESHEE, an old colored preacher in a Louisiana village, is teaching his Sunday School class the stories of the Old Testament. One by one his dramatic portrayals are brought before our eyes, beginning with a fish fry attended by a number of very practical masculine and feminine colored angels and cherubs, by Gabriel, and by the Lord God himself. Being in a miracle-working mood God decides to perform a real eye-opener and creates Earth. When this is done He sees that He must create a man to till the fertile fields he has made. Naturally the woman follows.

We are taken on through the story of Cain and Abel, the wickedness of the world which manifests itself before our eyes in drunkenness and crap shooting, and finally the cruise in the ark of a very human Noah. We are shown the scene in God's "office" in Heaven when he decides to choose one race of people on whom the salvation of the world shall rest . . . the descendants of Abraham, Isaac, and Jacob.

Follows the divine appointment of Moses and Aaron to lead the children of Israel from Egypt. The two leaders display their newly acquired "magic" before Pharaoh and his court, a display that culminates in the death of the eldest son of each Egyptian household.

Next we see the chosen race on the banks of the Jordan. We listen with Moses to the blast of Joshua's trumpet and the crumbling of the walls of Jericho. But finally even the chosen people lose favor in God's sight because of their wickedness. Jerusalem is about to be captured but God will not listen to the pleas of the Heaven-dwellers that he help in its defense. Finally, however, he is moved to go down to Earth and look things over for himself. His conversation with Hezdrel, captain of the city's defense, gives him a new light on God-

hood. The prophet Hosea, it seems, has taught people that God is a God of love and mercy and that through suffering they will be purified to be worthy of a place in His kingdom.

This new version of the redemption of man gives God serious thought. As the play closes with a second fish fry God looking down upon Earth filled with a sobering sense of responsibility sees a crucifixion and conceives the idea of saving mankind from sin through the sacrifice of a divine Son.

Philip Barry

··{ *Born, Rochester, New York, 1897* }··

ALL too frequently people who win prizes with a first play or first novel have their one brief moment and are never heard from again. Not so Philip Barry. When his play, *You and I*, won a $500 prize and Broadway production he was still a student in Professor Baker's famous "English 47" at Harvard, but his prize-winning play proved the stepping stone to a successful playwrighting career.

Strictly speaking, however, *You and I*, was not Barry's first attempt at dramatic art. When he was thirteen he wrote an involved discussion of reincarnation called *No Thoroughfare*. Needless to say, it found no thoroughfare to Broadway. Nor was his dramatic treatment of psycho-analysis under the same title written at twenty more successful. While at Yale, however, he wrote a one-act play, *Autonomy*, a bitter political satire, that was given as a curtain raiser, so to speak, for Yale's Pump and Slipper Dance. His fourth attempt was a farce written in professor Baker's Harvard "workshop" and called *A Punch for Judy*. This was subsequently played on tour by the Workshop Company.

During all this time he supported his interest in dramatic writing by various jobs, one in the State Department at Washington, another as a minor employee of the American embassy in London, still another as advertising copywriter. But with the financial success of *You and I* he was enabled to make playwriting his career. Followed *The Youngest* which achieved a moderate success. Then came three successive commercial failures: *In a Garden, White Wings*, and *John*, the last named being a sensitive and sincere Biblical drama dealing with the life of John the Baptist. But if these were financial failures, artistically they added to the stature and ability of the playwright so that when *Paris Bound* appeared in the season of 1927-28 the public hailed him with acclaim and said it at the box office window with dollars. This play was a smart and modern yet sane and fair discussion of the unfair importance attaching to adultery in a truly spiritual marriage.

Following the success of *Paris Bound* Barry and Elmer Rice collaborated on *Cock Robin* and Barry wrote *Holiday*, another box office hit. Then came *Tomorrow and Tomorrow*, rated by Robert Garland as the best of Barry's efforts to date. The latest Barry play to secure box office attention was *The Animal Kingdom*, a popular attraction of the season 1931-32. Barry, however, still holds *John* and *White Wings* his two best efforts.

Barry's family consists of a wife, two sons, a daughter and a dog. He confesses to a preference for working in Cannes, France, and says his hobbies are walking, swimming, and talking to whomsoever will listen.

TOMORROW and TOMORROW

Produced January 13, 1931, at the Henry Miller Theater, New York City.

SCENE: *A small Indiana town.*

GAIL and Eve Redman live in Redmanton, Indiana, the seat of Redman College. They appear happy except for the fact that six years of marriage have brought them no children. With Eve the fear that she may never have a child has become almost an obsession.

Into their peaceful routine comes Dr. Nicholas Hay, who has given up the practice of medicine for research and lecturing on psychiatry. Dr. Hay, who is to be the guest of the Redmans during his invitation lectures at the college, immediately senses some crying need within Eve that is slowly destroying her.

The two fall inevitably in love but no word is spoken until the night before Dr. Hay's departure for Europe. Eve has just confessed that she never walks by the river when the laurel is in bloom because the very magnitude of its beauty and fragrance overpowers her. Instantly Dr. Hay diagnoses her trouble and accuses her of being afraid of life. He says that only if she gives herself up completely to her emotions will she have a child. He challenges her to walk with him through the blossoming laurel.

. . . .

Christian Redman, Eve's eight-year-old son, does not share the Redman love of horses. He is being taught to ride and jump, however, and because he falters at a difficult jump, Gail tells Eve that their son is "yellow." His failure preys, too, on the boy's own mind. Scarcely recovered from a serious illness, he steals from the house, puts his horse magnificently over the difficult jump and returns to the stables to fall unconscious in the groom's arms.

When Dr. Hay had left Eve nearly nine years before, he had told her that if she ever needed him he would come. "But," he added, "you must be prepared to acknowledge our love and go with me." Now with her son at the point of death Eve feels that only Dr. Hay can save him. She locates the doctor in Chicago and he comes. He senses that Christian is his son. Love and skill combine to break through the boy's stupor and bring him back to life.

Dr. Hay reminds Eve of her promise. Although she is greatly tempted, she realizes the complete ruin it would make of her husband's life and is strong enough to refuse. Dr. Hay bows to her decision for, after all, have they not known in their complete surrender to each other the best that life has to offer?

DRAMA in the FIRST QUARTER of the TWENTIETH CENTURY

WITH the turn of the century the American stage came into its own. Broadway stood on an equal footing with London and Paris. And outstanding among the dramatists of the first decade of complete independence was Percy Mackaye whose *Scarecrow* would still furnish an excellent evening's entertainment. Then there was Charles Rann Kennedy, an Englishman living in New York, whose two dramas on religious themes, *Servant in the House* (1908) and *The Terrible Meek* (1911), were among the most discussed plays of their respective seasons. There was Israel Zangwill whose *Melting Pot* struck an entirely new note and created something of a furore in its day. There was the English success by Jerome K. Jerome, also religious in theme . . . that *Passing of the Third Floor Back* which probably owes its success more to the compelling personality of the actor, the late Sir Charles Forbes-Robertson, than to its dramatic excellence. And speaking of plays on religious themes, there was at a much later date Channing Pollock's excellent and entertaining drama, *The Fool*.

In the first quarter of the century there were also two outstanding biographical plays: the *Abraham Lincoln* created by the English playwright, John Drinkwater, and *Disraeli* by the English, Louis Parker.

In the matter of novelties two young playwrights, Hazelton and Benrimo, collaborated on a play, Chinese in theme, character, and manner of production, which they called *The Yellow Jacket* and which enjoyed production on innumerable foreign stages. In this classification, too, should be included Louis Parker's altogether charming *Pomander Walk*.

In England John Masefield wrote *The Tragedy of Nan;* Granville Barker produced the somewhat heavy social comedy, *Madras House*, the drama, *Waste*, and, in collaboration with Louis Housman, the poetic drama, *Prunella;* the novelist, Arnold Bennett, achieved in the collaboration, *Milestones*, his one dramatic success; and the dramatic critic, William Archer, refuted for all time the statement that dramatic critics are gentlemen who cannot write playable plays with his successful melodrama, *The Green Goddess*.

The first quarter century likewise brought success to several women playwrights: Lulu Vollmer with *Sun-up;* Susan Glaspell with her satire, *Suppressed Desires*, and whose drama, *Alison's House*, won the coveted Pulitzer Prize in 1930-31; Rachel Crothers with a long list of successful plays of which *Nice People* and *Expressing Willie* are perhaps the best; Zoë Akins with *Declassée* and Maurine Watkins with the first of the gangster plays, *Chicago*.

Then, too, there is Hatcher Hughes with his *Hellbent fer Heaven;* Owen Davis, who left civil engineering to become the Lope de Vega of the American stage and who travelled from the hack-drama of *Nellie, the Beautiful Cloak Model* to the Pulitzer-prize-winning *Icebound;* and Sidney Howard who really should be classified with . . .

Eva La Gallienne in Alison's House *by Susan Glaspell*

The STAGE of TODAY and TOMORROW

FOR the most part the playwrights of today are the playwrights of yesterday. Among current Broadway offerings that are rated high by first-string critics is *Accent on Youth* by that Samuel Raphaelson who has *The Jazz Singer* to his credit. It is described as a "light and literate comedy with an almost Oscar Wildean humor."[1] *The Children's Hour* by Lillian Hellmuth is rated the dramatic hit of the season. With a great deal of emotional appeal it deals with the mess made of two women teachers' lives by the unfounded and malicious charges of an adolescent girl. *The Petrified Forest* by Robert Sherwood with the inimitable Leslie Howard and plenty of gunfire is another outstanding success of the current season. It is from the pen of a dramatist who made his first success with *The Road to Rome* in the season of 1926–7. The important thing about the two last-named plays is not that they are successes but that both deal with themes that but yesterday were considered the exclusive property of psychiatrists and mental sanitariums. Their outstanding success will no doubt encourage other playwrights, for better of for worse, to dig up more of our queer mental quirks to supply themes for the plays of coming seasons.

Another signboard to the stage of tomorrow appears, some critics think, in the work of that new playwright, Clifford Odets, whose *Awake and Sing* and *Waiting for Lefty* are propaganda plays with a frankly reddish tinge. Mr. Odets is, nevertheless, looked upon by the critics as the only new material of promise the season has brought forth.

Maxwell Anderson may still be looked to for something worthwhile. And there is that Elmer Rice, born Reizenstein, whose *On Trial* was a dramatic innovation and whose *Street Scene* ranks him as an artist who may well be heard from once his fit of temperament is past. Nor among Americans of today can we forget the southerner, Paul Green, who in his play, *In Abraham's Bosom*, made a powerful presenta-

tion of a problem that will have to be reckoned with in the near future.

Four other tendencies deserve at least passing mention: First the spread of the "Little Theater" movement and a renewed box office interest in "the road"; second, an increasing tendency to revive successful plays of past generations and even of past centuries; third, an inclination in New York to form new non-commercial production groups such as the *Theater Union*, the *Theater Alliance* and the *Theater of Action;* and, finally, Gilbert Miller's prognostication (in the *New York Times*) that the day of the drawing-room play is over, that the drama of tomorrow will be "dedicated to airliners, hotels, four-day boats and the like."

There are those who mourn that the theater in America is dead . . . choked by commercialism. If the offerings of the current season represent theatrical death . . . long live the theater!

"The Old Maid," by *Zoe Akins. Pulitzer Prize Play, 1935.*

[1] Robert Garland in his contemporary dramatic column in *The World-Telegram*.